JAL
Japan Airlines
The Story of the Flying Crane

JOZEF MOLS

KEY
Books

AIRLINES SERIES, VOLUME 25

Published by Key Books
An imprint of Key Publishing Ltd
PO Box 100
Stamford
Lincs PE9 1XP

www.keypublishing.com

The right of Jozef Mols to be identified as the
author of this book has been asserted in accordance
with the Copyright, Designs and Patents Act 1988
Sections 77 and 78.

Copyright © Jozef Mols, 2025

ISBN 978 1 80282 922 8

All rights reserved. Reproduction in whole or in part
in any form whatsoever or by any means is strictly
prohibited without the prior permission of the
Publisher.

Typeset by SJmagic DESIGN SERVICES, India.

Contents

Introduction and Acknowledgements

With a population of more than 130 million people, spread over four main islands and thousands of smaller islands, Japan relies heavily on connectivity in its aim of building an economy in which exports play a major role. This was already anticipated in the first decades of the last century and, accordingly, Japan's first domestic airlines were established around 1923. In the 1930s, some of them would assist the government in its geopolitical objectives, such as the invasion of Manchuria. The following years would see the airlines become more and more involved in the World War Two effort until the Japanese capitulation in 1945 brought all aviation activities to a standstill.

It would be 1951 before Japan Airlines received permission to start up domestic flights, but the airline was not allowed to own aircraft. Therefore, Martin 2-0-2's and Douglas DC-4s were leased from American airline companies, together with flight crews. In 1952, JAL could operate its first international route, linking Tokyo with Manila.

On 1 August 1953, the Japan Airlines Limited Act came into effect, forming a new state-owned Japan Arlines that assumed all assets and liabilities of its private predecessor. In 1954, having received Douglas DC-6 aircraft, JAL opened its first intercontinental route, linking Tokyo with San Francisco via the Pacific Ocean. That year, JAL also introduced two seat classes: First Class and Tourist Class. Then, in 1960, the airline started up a northern route service to Europe. At the same time, further routes within Asia were developed and soon, the airline would acquire modern jets including the Douglas DC-8 and Convair 880.

JAL was not the only airline in Japan. Through private initiative, wars smaller airlines such as Far East Airlines, All Nippon Airways and Fujita Airways were established, but they soon merged into ANA All Nippon Airways, which would become JAL's major competitor. Government intervention through the Ministerial Resolution Concerning Airline Operations divided the market into segments in which JAL received a monopoly on international routes, whereas its competitor ANA was assigned domestic routes but was also authorised to operate international charter flights.

Deregulation would come only in the 1980s. In 1987, JAL was privatised. Stiffening competition from both domestic and international carriers resulted in downward pressure on profit margins, while both ANA and JAL needed to buy newer aircraft types such as the Boeing 747 and Douglas DC-10.

By the end of the decade the Japanese economy showed strong growth, and as a result the yen also appreciated considerably by comparison with foreign currencies. Holidays in Japan became more expensive for foreigners, however, so the number of international passengers declined and, following years of profit since 1986, JAL posted operating losses in 1992. In 1996, a major restructuring of the airline became necessary. However, since these measures were in sufficient, JAL looked at establishing worldwide relationships. The 9/11 terrorist attacks in New York and the SARS pandemic in 2003 further impacted the aviation sector. In 2002, JAL merged with JAS, a smaller domestic competitor.

The combination of the aftermath of the Gulf Wars of 2003 onwards, the swine flu pandem (2019) and the banking crisis in 2008 forced JAL to declare bankruptcy. In 2011, the carrier emerged from court-administered bankruptcy and could make a new start, but in the next decade would be confronted with the COVID-19 pandemic. Although the measures taken by the Japanese government during that worldwide event were less stringent than in many other countries, JAL suffered from a drop in passenger numbers and had to use part of its fleet to transport cargo. Even so, the airline resumed operations strongly after the emergency was over and its international bookings managed to return to pre-COVID levels.

The history of JAL is a fascinating one, especially for non-Asian readers. The way aviation developed in Asia is completely different from how it evolved in Europe and the USA. Airlines in Asia also have a different corporate culture, which makes studying their evolution both instructive and exciting.

I was only able to write the story of JAL Japan Airlines with the help of aviation historians, libraries, research institutions, specialised journalists and many photographers who provided the pictures that illustrate this book. Special thanks go to my partner, Marianne Van Leuvenhaege, who encouraged me while researching the subject and writing the book, and who was my first proofreader. Of course, my gratitude also goes to Key for publishing and distributing this book.

Jozef Mols
Wommelgem, Belgium
15 October 2024

Chapter 1

Early Pre-War Endeavours

Japan comprises 14,125 islands extending along the Pacific coast of Asia. It stretches 3,000km (1,900 miles) northeast–southwest from the Sea of Okhotsk to the East China Sea.[1] It will therefore not come as a surprise that this country was more than interested in the development of shipbuilding and the introduction of commercial aviation, not only to connect the different islands in the archipelago but also to stimulate trade with neighbouring countries in Asia.

On the morning of 5 December 1909, a bamboo-framed and white cloth-covered glider was towed, with a boy aboard, from the Daiichi Senior High School's athletic field. The glider was developed by Yves le Prieur, a military attaché at the French embassy in Tokyo, together with Lieutenant Aibara Shiro of the Japanese Navy and Professor Tanakadate Aikitsu of the Tokyo Imperial University's School of Science. It was Le Prieur himself who performed the first flight of his design four days later, which made him the first person to actually fly an aircraft in Japan.[2] Although the aircraft was fitted with an engine and a propeller, Le Prieur never attempted a powered flight.

In April 1910, the Japanese government decided to send two army officers, Hino Kumazō and Yoshitoshi Tokugawa, to France to train at the Henri Farman Aviation School at Étampes. When they returned to Japan, they both gave demonstrations with a German and a French plane they had purchased in Europe.[3] Around the same time, retired Japanese Navy engineer Sanji Narahara, who had studied munitions at the Imperial University, built an airframe for himself with which he made a successful flight on 5 May 1911. The aircraft was powered by a French engine. This was only seven and a half years after the Wright Brothers made the world's first powered flight on 17 December 1903.[4]

Besides French influence, American initiatives would also stimulate the appetite to further develop aviation. James 'Bud' Mars from Muskegon, Michigan, was known as a daring flyer in the USA. On 31 December 1910, he flew a Curtiss B-18 biplane for 3,000 (mostly) paying spectators in Honolulu, Hawaii. This was his first stop on the Curtiss Airplane Company's 3,000-mile demonstration tour, which included Japan, China, the Philippines, Siam, Singapore, Java, Persia, Africa, the Holy Land, Egypt, Spain, France and the United Kingdom. Mars was one of the first aviators to demonstrate flight in Japan, and even took the future emperor Hirohito (then 11 years old) on his first plane ride.[5] 'Bud' was surprised to find several aeroplanes in Japan, but discovered that they were all out of use because the officials did not understand the art of flying. As a result, impressed Japanese officials decided to start the production of aircraft in their own country instead of buying them from overseas.[6]

Japan was quick to see the military potential for aircraft as well as for civilian use, and construction of each type would go hand in hand. The genesis of Japanese-built aircraft can be traced back to the formation of the Provisional Military Balloon Research Association (PMBRA) initiated by an Imperial Order of 30 July 1909. Making up the organisation were 14 members from the Army, Navy, the Imperial University and the Central Meteorological Observatory. Day-to-day functioning of the organisation was influenced by the Army. The manufacture of aircraft, identified as Kaishiki (Association Type) aeroplanes, would continue until 1916. In 1911, Yoshitoshi Tokugawa designed and supervised the construction of the first Japanese-manufactured aeroplane, using a design from Henri Farman. It was built with Japanese cypress wood and covered with two layers of silk glued together by what was described as 'liquid rubber'. It would later be called the Kaishiki No 1, and made its first flight on 13 October 1911, piloted by Tokugawa himself. The confidence gained by the success of this plane resulted in the construction of four more aircraft of the same type, which were later supplemented by four imported Farman aircraft.

Now that training aircraft were available, the Army selected five officers to form the first class of pilot officers. In 1913, the Imperial Aeronautical Association was founded under the presidency of General Count General Nagaoka Gaishi. Between 1919 and 1922, it was responsible for organising airmail flying contests, during which the participants had to complete a course in the fastest time.[7] The third of these air races saw pilots fly from Tokyo to Osaka and back on 21 April 1920. The first prize was 10,000 yen and the second 8,000 yen, half of each prize being a gift from the Emperor. Two aviators out of the three entrants started the race; Mr Yamagata, flying an Itoh biplane with a 150hp engine, accomplished the flight of 630 miles non-stop in 6 hours and 39 minutes, thereby winning the first prize. Mr Jinuma, on a Nakajima biplane with a 210hp engine, lost control after 20 minutes of flying and came down in the neighbourhood of Mount Ōyama. Mr Okuri did not start.[8] Two years later, the fifth air race was organised over the same course. This time, 14 civilian pilots participated and the record time was reduced from 6 hours and 39 minutes to 4 hours and 49 minutes. This was a good measure of the progress accomplished.[9]

As aviation gained popularity, several entrepreneurs started up activities in this field. In January 1923, *The Asahi Shimbun* newspaper and Einosuke Shirato established the East-West Regular Transport Association the airline used former army Nakajima Type 5 aircraft, followed by Dornier Comets. At first, it offered only mail services, but with the arrival of the Comets, passenger flights between Tokyo and Osaka commenced in 1928.[10]

Meanwhile, Tamotsu Aiba, a well-known pioneer of Japan's automobile industry, started up a private flying school. A few years later, in September 1928, he established the Tokyo Air Transport Company (TAT). After obtaining approval for scheduled air services, it began operating flights between Tokyo and Shimoda with an Avro 504 seaplane, which, however, could only transport one pilot and one passenger. When the Navy sold its Brandenburg seaplane, TAT acquired it. The route from Tokyo to Shimoda was extended to Shimizu with two round trips per week. In 1931, mail services on the same route were introduced. In 1936, the airline recruited female pilots who had graduated from Aiba's flying school. Around the same time, more imported aircraft were added to the fleet. In 1939, however, when the Dai Nippon Airline Company Act was passed, air transport operations over distances of more than 300km (186 miles) were prohibited. Shortly afterwards, as the country moved towards wartime status, air transport operations were suspended in accordance with national policy.[11]

The Japanese government was also interested in the possibilities of regular passenger transportation. On 30 October 1928, the government established the Japan Air Transport Corporation (JAT) (Nihon Koku Yuso Kabushiki Kaisha) as the national flag carrier of the Ministry of Communications. The airline initially used the army air base at Tachikawa as its terminal in Tokyo before moving to Haneda Airport, which was completed in August 1931. JAT was heavily subsidised by the government, receiving the equivalent of $1 billion in today's currency. During the early 1930s, its aircraft were often used by the military for missions in Asia, especially during the invasion of Manchuria in 1931. The airline started up with a fleet of Fokker Trimotors, Fokker Super Universals and Nakajima Super Universals.[12] British Airspeed Envoys also arrived in Japan in 1935 and were used on the Urusan–Dairen route. Later on, Japan would obtain a manufacturing licence and Mitsubishi would build these aircraft, which were called Mitsubishi Hinazuru.[13] Under government pressure, East-West Regular Airlines was taken over by JAT.

The military transport missions in China by JAT declined as they were taken over by three new carriers that the airline helped to establish: Manchukuo National Airways in 1932, Huitong Airways in 1936 and China Airways in 1938. These subsidiary companies were joint ventures between JAT and the puppet governments of Manchukuo and the Provisional Government of the Republic of China. Manchukuo National Airways was by far the most important of the three subsidiaries. More than just a commercial airline, it engaged in a wide range of operations, including regular commercial passenger and cargo transportation, regular military transportation, mail transportation, charter flights, aerial surveying, aircraft maintenance and aircraft manufacturing. For its own needs, the airline designed and built the Manchuria Airlines MT-1, a passenger aircraft to be used on routes within Manchuria. Furthermore, it obtained aircraft from Germany in the form of the Junkers Ju 86, Heinkel He 116 and Messerschmitt Bf 108. From the USA, it obtained Lockheed Super Electras.[14]

As Manchukuo National Airways took over air transportation in Manchuria, JAT could now concentrate on the civilian passenger market in Japan and began to use the new 14-seat Douglas DC-2 on new, more commercially profitable routes between Japan and Manchukuo in 1936. With the start of the Second Sino-Japanese War in 1937, JAT benefited from a resurgence in military passenger traffic. In 1938, the airline carried nearly 323,000 passengers, representing 2.6 per cent of the world's passenger traffic. That year, the government established a new airline under the name Imperial Japanese Airways and JAT was merged into the new company.[15]

Renewed hostilities against China produced a tremendous need for air transport capability by the Japanese military, which had traditionally drawn on the resources of the civilian national flag carrier, Japan Air Transport, for its charter requirements. But JAT's capacity was limited, so conflict arose between the Imperial Japanese Army and the Imperial Japanese Navy over priority. The government saw the need for the creation of a single national monopoly. Therefore, it bought a 50 per cent share of Japan Air Transport and renamed it the Dai Nippon Koku (Imperial Japanese Airways, also known as Greater Japan Airways or Greater Japan Air Lines) in December 1938. The new airline continued to use the fleet of JAT, which was supplemented by Mitsubishi MC-20 transport aircraft plus domestically built versions of the 21-seat Douglas DC-3, some 500 copies of which were manufactured in Japan.

The beginning of the war in the Pacific in December 1941 profoundly affected Japanese commercial aviation. A month after the start of hostilities, the Japanese government suspended all commercial operations as aircraft were needed for the war. Thus, in 1941, the first era of Japanese commercial aviation effectively ended. It would take until 1951 before Japan could resume civilian air transport.[16]

A vintage black and white picture showing the first flight in Japan. (Jozef Mols collection)

Above left and above right: **Vintage posters of Japan Air Transport (JAT). (National Air and Space Museum – public domain)**

Below: **A 1935 timetable of Japan Air Transport (JAT). (Japan Air Transport – public domain)**

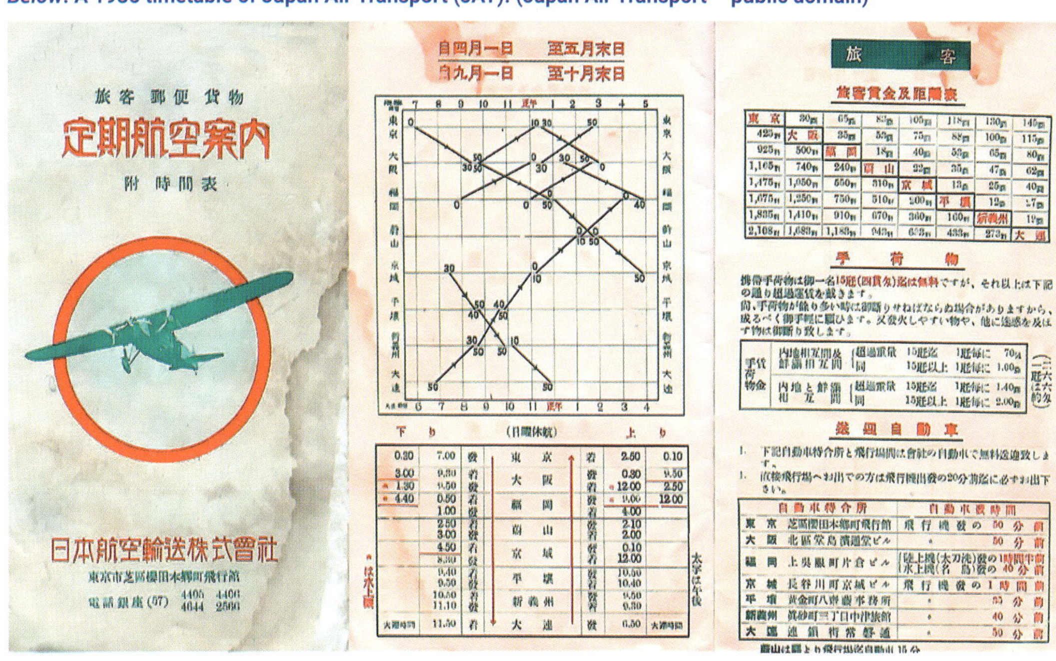

Above: A Japan Air Transport (JAT) Airspeed Envoy. (Jozef Mols collection)

Left: Dai Nippon Koku's (Imperial Japanese Airways) timetable December 1938 to March 1939. (Wikipedia – public domain https://en.wikipedia.org/wiki/File:Dai_Nippon_Koku.jpg))

A Manshu MT-1 Hayabusa, operated by Manchurian Airlines and built in Manchuria for the needs of the airline. (Creative Commons Attribution-Share Alike 4.0 International https://en.m.wikipedia.org/wiki/File:ManshuMT-1Hayabusa.jpg))

Above: Besides aircraft built in Japan, Manchukuo Airlines also operated some German aircraft including this Junkers Ju 86. (Bfd1942 GNU Free Documentation License, Version 1.2 https://commons.wikimedia.org/wiki/File:Ju86_Manchukuo.jpg))

Right: A Manchurian Airlines poster from the late 1930s.
(Jozef Mols collection)

Chapter 2

The Birth of Japan Air Lines

Once peace had returned, the American-led occupation of Japan added civil aviation to the ban on Japanese military pilots and planes. Simply put, no Japanese were allowed in the cockpit. Nobody could own an aircraft and no company could build an aeroplane or aircraft engine. Students couldn't study aeronautics, while teachers and engineers in the field had to find new jobs. Even gliding was banned. This ban, of course, was to prevent remilitarisation.[1]

In 1951, permission was granted to start up a domestic airline, but the airline would not be allowed to own aircraft. That year, potential investors gathered and applied for a licence to conduct domestic aviation services. Japan Airlines was granted this licence on 22 May 1951 and the company was formally established on 1 August. The initial capital amounted to 100,000 yen (at that time £735) represented by 2m shares, of which ten per cent was offered to the public. After setting up offices in different Japanese cities, the airline hired 15 stewardesses on 20 August 1951. In the meantime, Japan Airlines (JAL) had leased a Douglas DC-3 belonging to Philippine Airlines for a three-day period. The aircraft operated under the name *Kinsei*. This allowed some promotional trips to be offered to potential clients. On 11 October 1951, a consignment operation contract was concluded between JAL and Northwest Airlines as no Japanese pilots were licensed to fly passenger aircraft. A few days later, on 25 October, JAL launched the first civil aviation service in Japan since the end of the war. A Martin 2-0-2 named *Mokusei* with 36 seats connected Tokyo with Osaka via Fukuoka. This route would be flown once a day with American crew from Northwest Airlines. JAL would lease a total of five such aircraft from Northwest Airlines. From the start of its operations, JAL offered an in-flight-meal on all flights, which consisted of sandwiches in a paper box.[2]

On 2 November 1951, the airline received its first Douglas DC-4 ('Tenousei') which would, however, remain in the USA till 1952 for pilot-training purposes. Just like the Martins, this aircraft was leased from Northwest Airlines. In the meantime, several other Japanese cities such as Nagoya and Misawa were included in the network. In June 1952, the airline signed a contract for mail transportation with the Ministry of Post and Telecommunications. In July 1952, the Japan Airlines Maintenance Co Ltd was established, with a capital of 50m yen (£368,000). The first DC-4, leased in 1951, arrived in Japan on 1 September 1952, and was renamed *Tokachi*. It was immediately introduced on the Tokyo–Osaka–Fukuoka route. Two other aircraft of the same type had been ordered, the last of which arrived on 24 October 1952. This way, the Martin 2-0-2 could be retired. On 21 December 1952, JAL operated its first overseas flight between Tokyo and Manila, to send back the body of the Philippine Ambassador to Japan.[3]

On 1 August 1953, the Japan Air Lines Limited law came into effect, forming a new state-owned Japan Air Lines with a capital of 2 billion yen and which assumed all assets and liabilities of its private predecessor. On 2 October of the same year, JAL introduced the first DC-6B on the Tokyo to Sapporo route. JAL would use a total of ten aircraft of this type, which would soon form the backbone of its international fleet during the 1950s. A year later, on 2 February 1954, the same type of aircraft was introduced on the new Tokyo–Wake Island–Honolulu–San Francisco route on the basis of two round trips per week. Today, the flights between Tokyo and San Francisco still carry flight numbers 1 and 2 to commemorate this first international service, which was operated by American crews. The aircraft were serviced by United Air Lines in San Francisco. In April 1954, JAL introduced two seat classes: First Class and Tourist Class on its international routes. On 23 October 1954, two Japanese citizens acquired the first pilot licence (DC-4). On 2 November of that year, they were the first Japanese pilots to fly a commercial aircraft after the war (on the Tokyo–Fukuoka route).[4]

On 4 February 1955, JAL extended the Tokyo–Okinawa (Naha) route to Hong Kong, using its DC-6 aircraft. A year later, on 13 September 1956, the route was further extended to Bangkok and Singapore. In 1958, the airline introduced its first DC-7B on the route linking Tokyo with San Francisco via Honolulu. In 1959, two other Trans-Pacific routes were started between Tokyo and Los Angeles (via Hawaii with a DC-7C, and between Tokyo and Seattle via Anchorage, also with a DC-7C). A route linking Tokyo with Hong Kong now made a stop in Taipei. JAL would use a total of five DC-7Cs in the transition period, preceding the introduction of jet aircraft. This aircraft type was innovative, using turbo-compound engines to achieve higher speeds and longer range.[5] With the DC-7C, JAL was able to fly non-stop between Seattle and Tokyo in 1959.[6]

In April 1960, JAL started the Northern route service to Europe, linking Tokyo with Paris via Anchorage and Hamburg. The service was operated jointly with Air France, which made a Boeing 707 available for this operation. A few months later, JAL received the first jet of its own. The DC-8-32 was introduced on the route between Tokyo and San Francisco. Later, in November of the same year, the jet was also introduced on the Tokyo to Hong Kong route. JAL would operate a total of 51 DC-8 aircraft including DC-8-32, DC-8-33 and DC-8-53 types, the last of which was retired in 1987. By the end of 1961, the airline operated trans-polar flights from Tokyo to Seattle, Copenhagen, London and Paris via Anchorage. Trans-Pacific flights included Tokyo to Los Angeles and San Francisco via Hawaii. In 1962, after the delivery of Convair 880s (of which the company ordered nine), JAL also initiated flights to Europe via India. Earlier and for a short time only, the same aircraft were used on domestic flights between Tokyo and Sapporo. Also in 1962, the Tokyo–Singapore route was further extended to a Tokyo–Hong Kong–Bangkok–Singapore–Jakarta routeing, once again using the Convair 880. And in 1964, the Convair was also used to start up a Tokyo–Seoul route.[7] When JAL made the decision to obtain this type of mid-size jet, it intended to use it on South-East Asian routes and southerly routes to Europe, which had shorter interval distances and were not expected to have a high volume of passengers. On domestic routes, it was used to counter competition from turboprop aircraft.[8]

Hostesses in front of a JAL Douglas DC-3 on 27 August 1951. (Unknown author, public domain, https://en.wikipedia.org/wiki/Japan_Airlines#/media/File:Japan_Airlines_DC-3_Kinsei_PI-C7_Air_Hostesses_August_27_1951_Photo_1.png)

Left: As the Martin 2-0-2s were leased from an American airline, they kept an American registration number. (JAL)

Below: Martin 2-0-2s were used in the early days and were flown by Northwest Airlines' cockpit crews. (JAL)

Bottom: A JAL Douglas DC-4. These aircraft were also leased in the USA. (Alan Bushell)

Right: A JAL Douglas DC-6 in flight. (JAL)

Below: The Douglas DC-6B was the first JAL aircraft to fly intercontinental routes. (Alan Bushell)

Bottom: With the Douglas DC-7C, JAL inaugurated the Tokyo–Los Angeles route via Hawaii. (Alan Bushell)

Top: Throughout its history, JAL used many Douglas DC-8 jets of several subtypes. (JAL)

Above: Convair 880 jets were added to the fleet to supplement the DC-8 on shorter international routes and those with less passengers. (Alan Bushell)

Left: This old press photo shows JAL's Convair 880 in flight. (JAL)

Chapter 3

JAL and the Competition

Japan Airlines was not the only airline to start up activities in the early days of the post-war period. Nippon Herikoputa Yuso (Nippon Helicopter and Aeroplane) (NH) was founded on 27 December 1952, and in December 1953 commenced its first cargo flight between Osaka and Tokyo. Passenger services on the same route began on 1 February 1954, using a de Havilland Dove (JA5008). Then, in March of the same year, the service was upgraded to a de Havilland Heron. In 1955, Douglas DC-3s began flying for NH, by which time the airline's route network extended from Northern Kyushu to Sapporo. In December 1957, Nippon Helicopter changed its name to All Nippon Airways Company.[1]

Far East Airlines (Kyokuto Koku) was founded on 26 December 1952, one day before Nippon Helicopters, but it did not begin operations until 20 January 1954. It first started cargo runs between Osaka and Tokyo, also using a de Havilland Dove. It adopted the DC-3 in early 1957, by which point its route network extended through southern Japan from Tokyo to Kagoshima. When Nippon Helicopter changed its name to All Nippon Airways Company, Far East Airlines merged with the newly formed company. Furthermore, Fujita Airlines, formed in 1956, also merged into All Nippon Airways. On the other hand, Fuji Air Lines (formed in 1952) merged with Nitto Airlines (formed in 1955) to form Japan Domestic Airlines (JDA). North Japan Airlines (formed in 1962) also merged with JDA. Finally, Toa Airways (formed in 1953) merged with JDA.[2] Ultimately, JDA would merge with Japan Airlines in April 1964.

All Nippon Airways (ANA) would be the most important competitor for JAL Japan Airlines by far. In the 1960s, it added Vickers Viscounts to its fleet, followed a year later by Fokker F.27s. Competition on domestic routes was countered by JAL, which allocated its Convair 880 jets to the most important of these. In turn, All Nippon Airways sought to obtain Boeing 727 trijets for use on the Tokyo–Sapporo route. At first, the Japan Civil Aviation Bureau denied an import licence for ANA's 727s, unless Japan Airlines also acquired its own fleet of the same type.[3]

JAL introduced the trijet in 1965 and the model would remain in service until February 1988. In the meantime, the flag carrier had also obtained Douglas DC-8-55 jets, while for its domestic routes, JAL introduced the Japanese-built NAMC YS-11. Shortly afterwards, ANA introduced examples of the same type on its domestic routes, replacing its Convair 440s. JAL had simultaneously absorbed the Japan Aircraft Maintenance Company (JALCO), which performed maintenance service on its rapidly expanding fleet. In 1963, JAL established JALUX Inc., to handle the airline's procurement business. This was responsible for various work for the company, including the JAL Selection merchandise and in-flight meals and refreshments supplied to Blue Sky and JAL-DFS shops. Furthermore, aircraft fuel, cabin service and in-flight duty-free goods were also obtained via JALUX.

In 1963, JAL painted its fleet with the Tokyo Olympic mark to emphasise the airline's status as the official partner of the Summer Olympics, which took place in Tokyo in 1964. That year, JAL inaugurated the 'Sunset Express' service, linking Hong Kong and trans-Pacific destinations (Hong Kong, Tokyo, Honolulu–Los Angeles). As far as its sales policy was concerned, JAL started using electronic seat-reservation systems on international routes and introduced a cancellation fee on such flights. And in 1965, JAL started offering the first international travel packages in Japan (JALPAK). The same year, JAL established its headquarters in the Tokyo Building in Marunouchi, Chiyoda, Tokyo. By this time, more than half of JAL's revenue was generated on trans-Pacific routes to the United States, and the airline was lobbying in the USA for fifth freedom rights to fly trans-Atlantic routes from the East Coast. The trans-Pacific route, on the other hand, was extended east from San Francisco to New York in November 1966 and to London in 1967.[4]

Both JAL and ANA had listed their stock on the Tokyo Stock Exchange. In a move to protect government-owned Japan Airlines, the government granted JAL a monopoly on international scheduled flights that would last until 1986. However, ANA was allowed to operate international charter flights, the first of which took place on 21 February 1971 when a Boeing 727 flew the Tokyo to Hong Kong route. JAL then signed an agreement with Aeroflot to operate a joint service between Tokyo and Moscow, using a Soviet Tupolev Tu-114. The flight crew included one JAL member and the cabin crew had five members each from Aeroflot and JAL. These weekly flights started in April 1967.[5] When the agreement with Aeroflot ended in 1970, JAL started up an independent operation on the Tokyo–Moscow–Paris route as well as a Tokyo–Moscow–London service, each with DC-8s. As a result of its success on international routes, in a bold move JAL decided to order three Concorde supersonic passenger jets, but this order would be cancelled a few years later.

As explained above, the first years of civil aviation in post-war Japan saw a lot of airlines taking to the skies. Some of these were rather small and their business conditions unstable, so some bankruptcies and consolidations occurred. In December 1957, some of these smaller companies merged to form All Nippon Airways, which became the second major airline and a purely private carrier. After that, the remaining companies underwent various consolidations and by the mid-1960s, there were four major airline companies in Japan: JAL, ANA, Japan Domestic Airlines (JDA) and Toa Airways (TA). In the second half of the 1960s, TA developed co-operative arrangements with ANA, while JDA associated with JAL. As a result, it was assumed that the smaller two carriers would be consolidated into the big two (JAL and ANA).[6] However, demand for airline services rapidly increased in 1968–69. As profits surged, Toa Airways grew reluctant to be merged with ANA, while JDA refused to be acquired by JAL in 1970. Consequently, TA and JDA merged with each other to form Toa Domestic Airlines in 1971. This carrier would later change its name to Japan Air System. In response to these changing market conditions, the government changed its policy and issued the Cabinet Meeting Resolution 'Concerning Airline Operations' in November 1970 and the 'Notice from the Minister of Transport' in July 1972. The resolution of 1970 approved the change from a two-company regime (JAL and ANA) to a three-company regime (JAL, ANA and JAS). Furthermore, the ministerial notification of 1972 laid out specific rules pertaining to the business fields of the three airlines. These decisions are sometimes called the 'Aviation Constitution'. Under this constitution, the Japanese airline industry was segmented into different markets. JAL would serve international routes and domestic trunk routes, ANA would serve domestic trunk routes, local routes and short-distance international charter flights, and TOA Domestic Airlines would handle local routes and some domestic trunk routes. As for international air cargo, a new carrier could enter the market if there was enough demand. JAL was already operating cargo flights between Japan and San Francisco using DC-7F aircraft converted from DC-7Cs. Later on, in 1967, a DC-8-55F cargo freighter would be used on the same route. A few months later still, the same type of aircraft would also be used for cargo flights to New York via San Francisco and Honolulu. The changes in the government's approach to aviation resulted in the 1970–72 airline regulation system, which was intended to secure and nurture the transport capacities of all members of the industry by establishing a segmented business base for each firm.[7]

Despite offering a solid business base for the airlines, the government's policy produced unexpected repercussions. In the years following the Aviation Constitution, trunk-route markets such as Sapporo–Tokyo–Osaka–Fukuoka–Naha grew much faster than other local markets. As fares were set in proportion to flight distances, ANA and JAS began using their trunk routes to cross-subsidise those routes local routes that were in less in demand, suffering from deficits. Cross-subsidisation allowed each carrier to expand its route network without cut-throat competition and, at the same time, profits were protected for further investment, so this segmented-market approach allowed stable management and growth to be maintained. During the 1970s, the average growth rate of revenue-passenger-kilometres in the domestic market was 12.2 per cent, while the international market (where JAL had a monopoly) was an astounding 42.4 per cent. These high growth rates were the result of rapid growth of the economy and helped boost further network expansion.[8]

As a direct result of the high growth rate, Japan Airlines introduced the Boeing 747 in July 1970. This type started operations on the trans-Pacific routes to Honolulu and Los Angeles. In 1972, JAL was one of the first airlines to introduce non-smoking seats on its international 747 flights. After the jumbo jet took over the routes to the USA, the Douglas DC-8 aircraft that had previously operated the route was redeployed to open up new routes, such as to Mexico via Vancouver. In 1973, JAL started flights to Papeete (Tahiti) in a code-share agreement with Air France. A year later, flights to Rome and Frankfurt via Moscow were inaugurated, each time with a DC-8-62. The 747 would also be used within Japan on high-density domestic routes.[9] As this aircraft was very popular on these routes, JAL introduced the 747 SR in 1973. This was a short-distance version of the aircraft, offering a larger seating capacity, to be used on busy domestic routes.

In the meantime, Southwest Air Lines had been established in Okinawa. The founders of this new company wanted a piece of the rapidly expanding home market, although it never constituted a real threat to JAL. In fact, some years later, JAL would take over Southwest.

Above: Fuji Airlines was established in 1952 and operated domestic flights with Convair equipment. (Alan Bushell)

Right: Fuji Airlines merged with Nitto Airlines to form JDA. (Alan Bushell)

Above: North Japan Airlines (founded in 1962) also merged with JDA. (Alan Bushell)

Left: TOA Airways was incorporated in 1953 and offered domestic services. (Alan Bushell)

Below: Like most other early Japanese airlines, TOA also used Convair types for its domestic routes. (Alan Bushell)

ANA started operations with de Havilland Heron aircraft but soon obtained the Fokker F-27 Friendship. (Hideyuki KAMON CC BY-SA 2.0 https://commons.wikimedia.org/wiki/Category:JA01NV_(aircraft)#/media/File:CRF_F-27-050_(JA01NV)_@_MYJ_RJOM_(224940656).jpg))

ANA only received authorisation to import the Boeing 727 trijet on condition that JAL would obtain the same type of aircraft. (Pete Macklin - https://www.flickr.com/photos/161766398@N08/52937282637/ CC BY 2.0 https://commons.wikimedia.org/wiki/Category:JA8347_(aircraft)#/media/File:All_Nippon_Airways_Boeing_727-200_JA8347.jpg)

JAL introduced the NAMC YS-11 on its domestic routes in 1965. (Toshiyuki Toda via Jay Sherlock Collection)

Left: The Boeing 727-100 was introduced by JAL in 1965. This one, delivered in 1966, was obtained from Dan Air. (JAL)

Below: The 727-100 entered the JAL fleet, starting in 1965. (Jozef Mols collection)

Bottom: JAL used several subtypes of the Douglas DC-8, such as this DC-8-62H (Michel Gilliand, GFDL 1.2 - https://commons.wikimedia.org/wiki/Category:JA8053_(aircraft)#/media/File:McDonnell_Douglas_DC-8-62H,_Japan_Air_Lines_-_JAL_AN0723946.jpg)

A JAL Douglas DC-8-61 at Narita Airport. (Pete Macklin, CC BY 2.0 https://commons.wikimedia.org/wiki/Category:Douglas_DC-8_of_Japan_Airlines#/media/File:Japan_Airlines_DC-8-61_JA8042.jpg)

The Douglas DC-8 remained the backbone of JAL's long-distance fleet for a long time. (Jozef Mols collection)

JAL used the Boeing 747-SR with shorter range but more seat capacity on some busy domestic routes that required greater seat capacity. (Stuart Jessup, CC BY-SA 2.0 https://commons.wikimedia.org/wiki/Category:JA8119_(aircraft)#/media/File:BOEING_747SR-46,_JA8119_,_JAPAN_AIRLINES.jpg)

Left: A Boeing 747-100 seen at Hong Kong Airport in 1971. (wilford peloquin CC BY 2.0 https://commons.wikimedia.org/wiki/Category:JA8102_(aircraft)#/media/File:590a_Hong_Kong_airport_1971_(51320155407).jpg)

Below: For a while, JAL operated a code-share flight from Tokyo to Moscow, using an Aeroflot Tu-114. (Aeroflot)

Bottom left: A publicity poster, edited by Aeroflot to promote the code-share flights with JAL to Tokyo. (Aeroflot)

Bottom right: An Aeroflot Tu-114, used for the code-share service linking Moscow with Tokyo. (Aeroflot)

Right: After some time, the Tu-114 used on the code-share flights was replaced by an Aeroflot Ilyushin Il-62. (Aeroflot)

Below: Southwest Air Lines was JAL's newest competitor and set up shop in Okinawa. (Alan Bushell)

Bottom: In 1969, JAL started using the Beechcraft H18 for pilot training. (Alan Bushell)

When Politics Gets Involved

As both JAL and ANA rapidly expanded, each within its own market segment, several political factors would influence the management of these airlines. When the civil air treaty between Japan and the People's Republic of China was signed in 1974, Japanese airlines had to suspend their lucrative flights to Taiwan in exchange for rights on routes between Japan and China. However, JAL had a state-imposed monopoly on all international airline services from and to Japan, including those to Taipei. Therefore, it was decided to set up a wholly-owned subsidiary of JAL, which would take up the broken link by opening a route to Taipei in September 1975, whereas JAL itself would operate all flights to the People's Republic. (Later on, similar arrangements were made by Air France, British Airways, KLM, Qantas and Swissair for their services to Taiwan). Following negotiations between the Interchange Association in Japan and Taiwan's Association of East Asian Relations, Japan Asia Airways started flights to Taiwan on 15 September 1975. At first, the airline used Douglas DC-8 aircraft, followed later on by Boeing 747-100s (in 1982), Boeing 747-300s (in 1988), Boeing 767-300s (in 1997), and Douglas DC-10s (in 1986). All these aircraft were obtained on loan from parent JAL.

As JAL and ANA were rapidly growing, with an expanding network of flights, fleet management became an important issue. Both selected the Douglas DC-10 to add to their respective fleets. However, ANA unexpectedly cancelled its order with Douglas and instead decided to source Lockheed Tristars. As we know now, this decision was the result of corruption at the highest levels of international politics, which would lead to Japan's greatest postwar scandal and a major diplomatic incident that struck at the heart of Lockheed and US business practices. Lockheed's re-emergence as a civil airliner producer in the late 1960s had not been lucrative. In fact, the company had to accept a $250m (£199m) loan guarantee from the US government to avoid bankruptcy. The Tristar, though a fine and technologically advanced aircraft, had suffered due to its engine manufacturer Rolls-Royce's own near-bankruptcy. Besides, the aircraft had been designed as a medium-haul airliner, and therefore struggled to compete against the longer-range McDonnell Douglas DC-10. Lockheed was nowhere near selling the 300 Tristars it needed to break even and the oil crisis of 1973 had brought most potential customers to their knees. Convincing ANA to buy Tristars – although very difficult – was necessary.[1]

Bruce Aitken, a former employee of the CIA's predecessor, the OSS (Office of Strategic Services), was living in Guam at that time. Guam is a favourite holiday spot for Japanese tourists, especially those who play golf. Aitken was asked by Deak & Co (whose chairman, Nicolas Louis Deák, was a CIA operative) to transport a series of golf bags from Guam to Japan. These bags, conveniently, are great at storing large quantities of Japanese yen. After arriving in Japan, Aitken was met by a Catholic priest, to whom he handed the golf bags. The same operation happened a dozen times over the next two years, totalling many millions of American dollars. As it turned out, the Lockheed President Carl Kotchian had approved payments to Japan's Prime Minister Kakuei Tanaka, who then approached ANA chairman Tokuji Wakasa. Wakasa quickly agreed to turn the orders with McDonnell Douglas into orders with Lockheed, and ANA purchased 21 Tristars. Soon after Aitken's last trip to Japan, the Catholic priest was arrested. Investigations by the Japanese police made it clear that many mediators received a cash payout. Various players involved – including the Prime Minister – were arrested and tried in the following years.[2] One of the other people to be arrested was Yoshio Kodama, a distinctly unsavoury character. Heavily connected with organised crime, he had even been imprisoned for three years as a war criminal. Kodama pocketed about $7m (£5.5m) for his involvement which included sending gangs of thugs to disrupt ANA stockholder meetings, classic Yakuza extortion tactics, and slandering several high-ranking ANA managers.[3] JAL – although not directly involved – also became concerned and questioned its judgment for its own Douglas purchases? or questioned why the other company would cancel its Douglas order? Why did members of the board who had previously supported the purchase of the Douglas DC-10 suddenly change their mind in favour of the Tristar? Anyhow, JAL decided in the end to obtain the Douglas jets, and several of them were later used by JAL's new subsidiary Japan Asia Airways. JAL itself used the DC-10s on domestic routes linking Tokyo with Sapporo and Fukuoka. Later on, these aircraft were also used on the Tokyo to New York route via Anchorage, whereas the 747s allocated to these routes could now be used on the new route to Frankfurt via Copenhagen and, in 1978, also on flights to Honolulu. That year, JAL expanded non-smoking to all domestic and international flights. 1978 also saw a route from Tokyo to Saipan and Guam started, as well as a flight linking Japan with São Paulo and Rio de Janeiro. Thanks to succesful lobbying, the airline obtained fifth freedom rights between New York and São Paulo and between Vancouver and Mexico City.[4] JAL had already introduced B-747-F exclusive cargo freighters on its trans-Pacific routes in 1974. JAL Cargo was set up in 1979 by the same shareholders that had set up JAL.

In 1981, JAL commenced flights between Jeddah and Tokyo. Two years later, the first Boeing 747-300 arrived; on 15 December 1983 it was introduced on the trans-Pacific route. By the end of the year, the last DC-8s could be retired. The first Boeing 767 was delivered on 17 August 1985, and these would guarantee domestic services between Tokyo and Fukuoka, as well as international connections between Tokyo and Seoul. In 1986, JAL inaugurated a direct Nagoya–Honolulu route, followed by direct flights between Tokyo and Paris. This marked the first time that a commercial route had been established over Siberia to Europe.[5]

A JAL Boeing 747-146B (SR/SUD). JAL incorporated the -300 series stretched upper deck on some of their late-build B747-100s built for use on high-density domestic services. KLM was the only other airline to modify its 747-200 aircraft to SUD-standard. The paint scheme on this plane was applied after it had been introduction into service. (contri from Yonezawa-Shi CC BY-SA 2.0 https://commons.wikimedia.org/wiki/Category:JA8170_(aircraft)#/media/File:Japan_Airlines_Boeing_747-146B_(SR_SUD)_(JA8170_22390_636)_(6387836601).jpg)

Left: A Boeing 747-300, seen at Jakarta Soekarno Hatta International Airport in Indonesia. (Jozef Mols)

Below: Japan Air Lines Boeing 747-200. (contri from Yonezawa Creative Commons Attribution-Share Alike 2.0 Generic https://commons. wikimedia.org/wiki/File:Japan_ Airlines_Boeing_747-246B_ (JA8104-19823-116).jpg)

Bottom: JAL Cargo mainly used Boeing 747-200s, some of which were leased. (Jozef Mols)

Right: Douglas DC-10-40. (FotoNoir Creative Commons Attribution-Share Alike 2.0 Generic https://commons.wikimedia.org/wiki/File:Japan_Air_Lines_DC-10-40_(JA8531_216_46923)_(9474597487).jpg)

Below: JAL's subsidiary Japan Asia used JAL's DC 10-40 on routes to Taiwan in order to circumvent political problems when flying to China. (Jozef Mols collection)

Bottom: JAL introduced the Boeing 767-300ER in 1985. (Jozef Mols collection)

Chapter 5

Deregulation of Air Traffic

The government resolution of 1970 divided the Japanese aviation market between the main competitors, JAL, ANA and JAS. JAL would serve international routes and some local trunk routes, while ANA would offer domestic flights, local flights and long-range international charter flights. Air fares were set in proportion to flight distances, while the airlines started to use their trunk routes to cross-subsidise their deficit-ridden local routes. It may be argued that the segmented market approach was successful, since the internal cross-subsidisation allowed each carrier to expand its route network without cut-throat competition, protect profits for reinvestment and maintain stable management and growth.[1]

Not mentioned in the resolution of 1970 were international cargo routes. When ANA, in response to rapid growth in international air cargo transportation, applied to enter the international cargo market by forming Nippon Cargo Services (NCA), together with some shipping and moving companies, the application was not a challenge to the old regime. However, in order to establish international cargo flights in the United States, the Japan–US bilateral agreement had to be renegotiated. The Japanese government defended ANA's application by stating that NCA's flights should be allowed to enter the market to rectify an imbalance in the treaty. At that time, only one Japanese carrier was allowed to operate in the USA, whereas three American airlines had access to Japanese airports. The USA, however, seized the opportunity to demand an expansion of US-Japanese passenger services. By the mid-1980s, American domestic airlines had gone through revolutionary changes due to deregulation, as was clear by the rise of United Airlines, American Airlines and Delta Airlines as well as the decline of PanAm and TWA. These changes would spill over to the international network. By holding NCA's approval 'hostage', the USA succesfully negotiated the entry of Delta and American into the Japanese market. As ANA would be allowed to operate international cargo services, JAL wanted to rapidly expand its own non-trunk domestic routes. In September 1985, Japan's minister of transport and the Council for Transport Policy issued an interim report, followed by a final report in June 1986. The reports emphasised the need for change and for greater competition in both domestic and international markets. They advocated a new aviation policy that would include more international routes served by multiple carriers, competition on domestic routes to be promoted through new entries into particular city-pair markets, and the complete privatisation of Japan Airlines. At the same time, the Council for Transport Policy argued that American-style deregulation would not suit the Japanese market.[2]

There were clear differences between the American and Japanese markets. The Japanese domestic airline market, with about 78 million passengers, was one-sixth the size of the American market in terms of passenger numbers. Japanese airlines carried about 11 million international passengers per year, a quarter of the number transported by American airlines. Even so, while the Council for Transport Policy and the Japanese government endeavoured to design and implement a new aviation policy, the Japanese market rapidly expanded. From 1985 to 1991, passenger miles in domestic markets grew at the rate of 9.3 per cent annually, but growth dropped to only 3.4 per cent between 1991 and

1993. International markets still saw a growth of some 4.8 per cent. Operating profits of Japanese carriers followed the domestic traffic patterns, soaring to record highs in 1989 and declining from 1990 onwards. JAL was particularly hard hit, not only by slower growth but also by price competition and the effect of the appreciation of the Japanese yen; this hurt international routes that accounted for more than half of its operations. Ultimately, the Japanese government made few changes to the rules regulating domestic routes. Previously, traffic authorisations on a specific route were given to one airline only. Although the government now wanted to encourage competition, entry into domestic routes by a second airline would only be allowed when the number of passengers travelling annually on a specific route exceeded a certain threshold. The designation of a second carrier and the number of flights alloted to the two carriers on a double-tracked route were strictly regulated by the Ministry of Transportation. In certain cases, this was necessary due to capacity limitations at Tokyo International (Haneda) Airport and Osaka International (Itami) Airport. Price competition between two carriers serving the same route was nearly impossible as fares were set according to the distance, irrespective of other factors such as season or the price elasticity of demand.

Though the new aviation policy was heralded by the Japanese government, of more significance by far was the privatisation of JAL, which took place on 18 November 1987. Although the airline had been the designated national flag carrier since 1972, it would now have to compete with All Nippon Airways and Japan Air System (JAS) on both domestic and international routes. Increased competition resulted in changes in the airline's corporate structure, by which it was reorganised into three divisions: international passenger services, domestic passenger services, and cargo and mail services. The fleet was also reorganised, with examples of the Douglas DC-8 and Boeing 727 retired. With stiffening competition, JAL embarked on a series of code-share agreements to share risks with major airlines around the globe. In 1986, the airline had entered into such an agreement with Qantas on two routes, Tokyo–Perth and Tokyo–Brisbane. In 1988, an agreement was signed with Thai Airways on the Nagoya–Bangkok route, followed in 1989 by a code-share with Canadian Airlines on the Tokyo–Toronto flights. The previous agreement with Qantas was then extended to add the Tokyo–Adelaide–Melbourne route. February 1990 saw the arrival of the first Boeing 747-400, which was introduced on international flights between Tokyo and Seoul and also on domestic routes such as Tokyo–Fukuoka and Tokyo–Okinawa.[3]

Competition resulted in downward pressure on profit margins, so JAL set up Japan Air Charter (JAZ) on 5 October 1990. The new airline was 80 per cent owned by JAL and its operations included scheduled and non-scheduled international passenger services on 15 high-density/low-yield tourist destinations such as Hawaii and Thailand. Four Douglas DC-10 aircraft and later five Boeing 747 jets were used, all wet-leased from JAL. Cockpit crews were American contract pilots based in Hawaii and its cabin crews were hired and based in Bangkok, where the airline operated a cabin-crew training centre. Japan Air Charter operated its first international charter flight on 22 February 1991, flying from Japan to Hawaii. In October of the same year, the airline changed its name to JALways. In 1999, the carrier would obtain its certificate to operate scheduled services. Then, in 2001, JALways would become a wholly-owned subsidiary of JAL through an exchange of shares.

In order to train future pilots, JAL established J-Air Co Ltd in August 1989 as a flight training school subsidiary under the name of JAL Flight Academy (JFA). It provided conversion training for its flight engineers to become pilots. In April 1991, a new division of JFA was created to operate scheduled services in western Japan, where it succeeded the troubled Nishi Seto Airlink Services, a commuter airline serving this area. It introduced the 19-seat Jetstream 31, replacing the Embraer EMB 110 Bandeirante inherited from Nishi Seto. In 1996, JFA would be restructured and J-AIR was separated as a wholly owned regional subsidiary of JAL.

The growth in demand for international air transportation forced JAL to introduce larger widebody aircraft types, such as the Boeing 747-400. (Jozef Mols collection)

In 1990, JAL introduced the Boeing 747-400 on international and domestic routes. (Jozef Mols collection)

Left: A JAL Boeing 747-400, seen at the international airport in Zurich. (Jozef Mols collection)

Below: J-Air started up services in western Japan with the 19-seat Jetstream 31 (Contri, Creative Commons Licence CC BY-SA 2.0 https://en.wikipedia.org/wiki/J-Air#/media/File:J-AIR_BAe_3217_Jetstream_Super31_(JA8865_981)_(4080605968).jpg)

J-Air inherited Embraer EMB 110 Bandeirantes from defunct Nishi Seto Airlink Services. (Jozef Mols collection)

When ANA set up Nippon Cargo Airlines, the Japanese government had to adapt its aviation policy. (Jozef Mols collection)

Right: In order to counter pressure on profit margins, JAL set up JALways, which would fly high-density/low-revenue routes such as to Bangkok and Hawaii. The airline used the Douglas DC-10-40 on wet lease from JAL. (Jozef Mols collection)

Below: As a result of deregulation, JAL had to compete with other Japanese carriers including JAS. (Jozef Mols collection)

Chapter 6

Ups and Downs

By the end of the 1980s, the Japanese economy experienced strong growth. As a result, the yen also appreciated considerably in comparison with other foreign currencies and holidays in Japan became too expensive for many foreign tourists. At the same time, Japan Airlines could not sufficiently increase its air fares for travel originating overseas to match the appreciation of the yen. Therefore, overseas income, once converted into yen through the consolidated bookkeeping of JAL, was lower. The airline also encountered other economic difficulties as a result of recessions in the United States and the United Kingdom.[1] After the invasion of Kuwait by Iraqi forces in 1990 and the subsequent First Gulf War, passenger numbers dropped further and fuel prices went up. In a separate government action, JAL had to operate several special flights to evacuate Japanese citizens from the war zone.

Following years of profit since 1986, the airline began to post operating losses in 1992, and had to search for cost-cutting expedients. Japan Asia Airways, originally set up by JAL to operate flights to Taiwan, started a route from Nagoya via Saipan to Guam, but most low-profit routes were taken over by Japan Air Charter (JAZ). Tourism activities, such as the production and sales of holiday packages, were transferred to JALways. In 1994, JAL introduced the McDonnell-Douglas MD11 – called the J-Bird – on domestic flights, but also on regional flights to Jakarta and Denpasar, and later on, even to Delhi.[2]

In 1997, seven Boeing 737-400s were introduced on local routes. As JAL had little experience with this type of aircraft, JAL Express Co Ltd (JEX) was established to operate them. As one of the measures to counter financial difficulties, JEX would operate the domestic and regional flights with JAL equipment under a wet-lease agreement. The airline operated with non-Japanese cockpit crews and short-term contracted cabin attendants known as Sky Cast, who were also responsible for cleaning the aircraft between flights to reduce costs. Maintenance of the aircraft was carried out by Japan Trans Ocean (the new name of Southwest Airlines), in which JAL had a majority shareholding.

In the meantime, JAL was expanding and re-organising its route network. In March 1991, a Tokyo (Narita)–Washington service was introduced and in July, a Hiroshima–Seoul route (with a Boeing 767) was opened. In November, a year after the reunification of East and West Germany, JAL commenced a Tokyo–Frankfurt–Berlin route, using Boeing 747-300 aircraft. At much the same time, J-AIR inaugurated Hiroshima–Komatsu and Hiroshima–Nagasaki flights. In March 1992, JAL started its Osaka–Cairns–Sydney connection, followed by an Osaka–Bangkok route with DC-10s. One of these flights was extended to Singapore. In August of the same year, a Nagoya–Beijing route was opened, also using DC-10s. Later on, a Tokyo–Munich flight with Boeing 747-400s was added to the timetable.

The marketing department of JAL came up with some significant initiatives. First of all, on certain USA-bound flights, a sushi bar was introduced in First Class. In January 1993, the JAL SKY PLUS campaign was launched and, a month later, the airline opened a reservation centre for priority guests, intended for use by handicapped people. In April, the JAL Foundation and JAL began regular observation of the upper atmosphere by aircraft equipped with automatic atmosphere-sampling systems, in co-operation with the Meteorological Agency. In August, JAL introduced the first 'JAL Dream Express' aircraft, with Mickey Mouse and friends painted on the fuselage. The plane was used on the Tokyo–Sapporo and Tokyo–Fukuoka routes as a result of JAL becoming the official airline of Disneyland Tokyo. JAL determined that Disney characters, well-known and popular among people of all ages, could stimulate demand for family travellers. The design was based on white, with the aircraft representing the clouds, while the upper half was coloured light blue to represent the sky. It features illustrations of Mickey Mouse, Minnie Mouse, Goofy, Huey, Dewey, Louie, Pluto, Daisy Duck and Donald Duck, as well as Cinderella's castle at the rear. Disney characters were also featured in the interior and on the flight attendants' uniforms. The vertical stabiliser shows the 'Disney on Tour' emblem, which features an illustration of Mickey Mouse as a tourist.[3] In April 1994, JAL achieved a world's first with the introduction of the Sky Massage Seat, available to First Class passengers only on two international routes. In June 1995, JAL opened its website ahead of other airlines in Japan and started to provide interactive services.

Following the opening of the new Osaka Kansai International Airport, Japan Asia Airways inaugurated a flight from Osaka to Denpasar and Jakarta, using its Douglas DC-10. JAL, on the other hand, started up a route from Sendai to Honolulu – also with a DC-10, by wet-lease agreement from Japan Air Charter (JAZ). By the end of the year, an Osaka–Ho Chi Minh City route was added. At the beginning of May 1995, JAL took over the Nagoya–Okinawa route and the Nagoya–Yamagata rote from Japan Transocean Air. Then, in 1996, JAL commenced an MD-11-flown service between Osaka and Delhi, followed shortly afterwards by a twice-weekly Osaka–Milan–Rome, operated with a Boeing 747-400.

In October 1995, JAL hired its first female 'first grade aircraft mechanic' and in September 1997 as in September 1997, the first female pilot operated a Boeing 747 on the Tokyo–Hakodate route in the co-pilot's seat. JAL made headlines with other innovations; in November 1995, Japan Asia Airways applied pictures, designed by elementary and junior high school children from Taiwan, on the fuselage of one of its aircraft. In early 1996, the airline introduced the first international cargo freighter (a Boeing 747) painted with the logo of 'JAL SUPER LOGISTICS', on the Tokyo–Singapore route. A few months later, the airline expanded its offering of flights to Hawaii by adding a Tokyo–Kona–Honolulu service to its network. The same year, JAL introduced the 'SEASONS' concept to JAL Executive Class as part of the renewal of this service. Aircraft received new seats and passengers were offered new in-flight meals. Furthermore, they could use airport lounges. In December 1997, a JAL aircraft brought the Olympic Flame from Athens to Tokyo, and in early 1998, the airline displayed a logo supporting the Japanese team in the World Cup.

In 1994, JAL introduced the McDonnell Douglas MD-11. (Jozef Mols collection)

Above: **A McDonnell Douglas MD-11 'J-Bird' seen at the Singapore International Airport. (Jozef Mols)**

Left: **A McDonnell Douglas MD-11 'J-Bird' seen at the Soekarno-Hatta International Airport in Jakarta. (Jozef Mols)**

Below: **JAL Express (JEX) operated the Boeing 737-400 fleet on behalf of JAL. (Jozef Mols collection)**

JAL started an international freight service, linking Japan with Singapore. The Boeing 747 used on this route received the 'Super Logistics' logo. (contri, Wikimedia commons licence CC BY-SA 2.0 https://commons.wikimedia.org/wiki/Category:Japan_Airlines_fleet_(1989_livery)#/media/File:Japan_Airlines_Boeing_747-246F_(SCD)_(JA8171_23391_654)_(5742500784).jpg)

In co-operation with Disney, JAL painted this Boeing 747 in a special livery featuring Disney characters. (contri, Wikimedia Commons CC BY-SA 2.0 https://commons.wikimedia.org/wiki/Category:JAL_Dream_Express?uselang=ja#/media/File:Japan_Airlines_Boeing_747-146B_(SR_SUD)_(JA8170_22390_636)_(6387836601).jpg)

This Boeing 767-300 also received a special Disney livery. (Spaceaero2 Creative Commons CC Attribution-ShareAlike 3.0 https://ja.wikipedia.org/wiki/JAL%E3%83%89%E3%83%AA%E3%83%BC%E3%83%A0%E3%82%A8%E3%82%AF%E3%82%B9%E3%83%97%E3%83%AC%E3%82%B9#/media/%E3%83%95%E3%82%A1%E3%82%A4%E3%83%AB:JAL_dreamexpress_B767-300_MYJ.jpg)

Japan Transocean Airliner performed feeder services for JAL, which took over some of them at a later date. (Jozef Mols collection)

Chapter 7

The New Millennium

In the late 1990s, JAL prepared to enter the new millennium. The airline had experienced some setbacks, so measures to counter the decrease in income were necessary.

In 1996, JAL introduced its first Boeing 777-200 out of an order for ten of these jets. In July 1998, the airline would also receive its first Boeing 777-300, configured to carry 470 passengers (18 in first-class superseats and the remainder in economy). JAL planned to use the aircraft on domestic routes. It had been one of the launch customers for the 777-300 and had participated in the design phase of both the 777-200 and 777-300.[1]

During the 1996 restructuring, JAL had decided to separate J-Air from the JAL Flight Academy, and the regional carrier would now operate as a fully-owned subsidiary of JAL, serving mainly regional routes from Hiroshima Nishi airport.

Route expansion was another means of improving income. In 1998, JAL commenced a Nagoya–London route, followed by a Tokyo–Las Vegas route and a Niigata–Honolulu flight. In 1999, the Osaka–Chicago route was introduced as well as a cargo flight from Seoul to Osaka. The same year, JAL introduced 'JAL Online' software, which supported direct domestic ticket computer reservations and purchasing, targeting corporate customers.

However, these measures were not enough to substantially increase profits. Observing other airlines' formation of worldwide relationships, JAL looked into setting up such arrangements of its own. In the passenger sector, JAL entered into agreements with American Airlines, British Airways, Swissair and Cathay Pacific, while Lufthansa Cargo and Singapore Airlines began to co-operate in the cargo market.[2]

Another definer of Japan's modern air transportation markets was deregulation. New airlines had entered the field and it was predicted that these would soon have the freedom to enter and withdraw from routes as they wished,[3] which would spark more competition.

In 1997, Japan Airlines' competitor JAS set up Hokkaido Air System Co Ltd. This was a joint venture between the Hokkaido government and regional municipalities, and was an affiliate of Japan Air System.[4] JAS also set up Harlequin Air Co with headquarters at the Fukuoka airport in Hakata-Ku, in order to operate regional flights.[5]

Skymark Airlines was formed in November 1996 as an independent domestic airline after deregulation of the industry and started operations on 19 September 1998. It was originally owned by a consortium of investors, led by the travel agency H.I.S. and leasing company Orix. Takashi Ide, the former head of British Airways in Japan, was hired as the company's CEO. At first, Skymark operated from Itami airport in Osaka, but later moved to Tokyo. The airline used a fleet of Boeing 767s, dry-leased from All Nippon Airways. For JAL, this came as a blow, as Skymark was the first low-cost airline established in Japan.[6]

Another airline, Air Do, was also of concern for JAL. Air Do would indeed become the second Japanese low-cost carrier and would co-operate with All Nippon Airways (ANA) from its hubs in New Chitose airport in Sapporo and Haneda airport in Tokyo. The airline was founded in 1996 by Teruo Hamada, shortly after the Japanese government approved a domestic airline deregulation policy that allowed carriers to set their own fares on domestic routes. The airline operated its first flight on the Tokyo–Sapporo route in December 1998 with a fleet of Boeing 767s. Maintenance of the fleet was subcontracted to Japan Airlines. At first, the new airline had high load factors, as fares were 30 to 40 per cent lower than those charged by other airlines on the same routes. Other airlines, including Japan Airlines, had to follow and discounted their fares as well, leading to pressure on profit margins. Even so, load factors on Air Do subsequently dropped to some 50 per cent. Following the 9/11 events in New York and a sanction from the Japanese government in 2014 (for promoting a first officer to captain despite poor performance in training), Air Do ran into financial difficulties.[7]

JAL, of course, had to react to the entrance of new carriers. In a first move, it had already established J-Air as an independent airline within the JAL group after cutting its ties with the Japan Airlines Flight Academy. By 2000, J-Air would receive the first of its modern Bombardier CRJ-200 jets. Subsequently, JAL set up Amakusa Airlines in 1998 to operate regional services from the Amakusa airport with de Havilland Canada DHC-8-100s. Although the municipal government of Amakusa had an 80 per cent stake in the new carrier, JAL effectively controlled its day-to-day operations.[8]

Just after the start of the new millennium, Boeing announced that JAL had placed an order for eight Boeing 777-200ERs and three 767-300ERs, to replace JAL's fleet of ten McDonnell Douglas MD-11s. The 767s would also be a better fit with the new second runway at Narita airport outside of Tokyo, scheduled to open in the summer of 2002. The value of the new aircraft at list prices was estimated at $1.6 billion (£1.243bn). The MD-11s would be traded in to Boeing, which would convert them to cargo freighters for United Parcel Service. JAL estimated that replacing the MD-11s with the new aircraft would improve the JAL group's cash flow by approximately $100m (£77.7m) annually; the operating costs of the 777-200ER would be comparable to the MD-11 while providing greater range and seat capacity. The 767-300ER, on the other hand, would provide lower operating costs than the MD-11 and would be used on the airline's medium and short-range international routes. The aircraft would be able to fly non-stop from Tokyo to Sydney, whereas the 777-200ER would allow JAL to operate non-stop services between Japan and America's East Coast.[9] In 2001, JAL would order another three Boeing 777-200ERs.

In a move to attract further attention, JAL launched the 'JAL Dream Express 21' livery in 2001.[10] The project was launched to commemorate the 100th anniversary of Walt Disney's birth, the 50th anniversary of Japan Airlines and the opening of Tokyo Disney Sea, of which JAL was the official sponsor. A total of six Boeing 747-400s was selected, five for domestic routes and one for international routes. The fuselage of these aircraft was inscribed with 'Walt Disney 100 Yyears of Magic'; the vertical stabiliser was painted wine red with 'JAL 50th Anniversary' written on it, and the silhouettes of a Martin 2-0-2 and a Boeing 747-400 were included. Boeing 747-100 JA8908 was treated to the 'Friends' livery, with a white base colour and the characters of Pluto, Goofy, Donald Duck, Daisy Duck, Huey, Dewey and Louie depicted. JA8904, meanwhile, received the mainly pink 'Sweet' livery, showcasing love stories such as *Aladdin, Cinderella, The Little Mermaid, Beauty and the Beast* and *Peter Pan*. The 'Family'-themed jet, JA8083, was mainly in blue with pictures of Bambi, Pinocchio, Dumbo and the 101 Dalmatians painted over the fuselage. The 'Tokyo DisneySea' jet, JA8912, was the fourth themed aircraft and the only one in international service, though JA8905 received the same painting. Finally, JA8084 received the 'Dream Story' painting in base yellow; its overall design was submitted by the public.

Though Walt Disney's characters might have had an impact on JAL's image, Disney's 'magic' was not able to solve the carrier's most important problems in a deregulated market, stung by a global downturn in travel. By the end of 2001, rumours spread that JAL and JAS (the smallest of the three major Japanese airlines) had started talks about a possible merger.

Above: In 1996, JAL introduced the Boeing 777-200. (Japanbird, wikimedia commons licence CC BY-SA 4.0 https://commons.wikimedia.org/wiki/Category:JA007D_(aircraft)#/media/File:JA007D_(aircraft)_Ukishima-cho_Park.jpg)

Left: A Boeing 777-200 with the JAL SKY NEXT logo. (Masahiro Takagi, wikimedia commons licence CC BY 2.0 https://commons.wikimedia.org/wiki/Category:JA007D_(aircraft)#/media/File:Japan_Airlines,_Boeing_777-289,_JA007D_(25628082746).jpg)

A JAL Boeing 777-200 landing at Osaka airport. (BriYYZ, wikimedia commons licence CC BY 2.0 https://commons.wikimedia.org/wiki/Category:JA008D_(aircraft)#/media/File:Japan_Airlines_Boeing_777-200_JA008D_(9964230543).jpg)

JAL Boeing 777-300. (Alan Wilson, wikimedia commons licence CC BY-SA 2.0 https://commons.wikimedia.org/wiki/Category:JA751J_(aircraft)#/media/File:Boeing_777-346_%E2%80%98JA751J%E2%80%99_Japan_Airlines_(47617068321).jpg)

Hokkaido Air System was set up by JAS in 1997 and operated Saab 340 aircraft. (Jozef Mols collection)

Right: A McDonnell Douglas MD-84 of Harlequin Air. The company was established by JAS and was therefore a competitor of JAL. (Amayagan, creative commons licence CCO public domain https://commons.wikimedia.org/wiki/Category:JA8552_(aircraft)#/media/File:HarlequinAir_MD-81_fukuoka_20041003113216.jpg)

Below: Skymark was formed in 1996 and started competition with JAL with a fleet of Boeing 767 aircraft, dry-leased from ANA. (Jozef Mols collection)

Above: Hokkaido International Airlines, better known under the 'Air Do' brand name, was an independent low-cost carrier in Japan, which disturbed the market by offering very low airfares. (Jozef Mols collection)

Left: JAL added the Bombardier CRJ-200 to J-Air's fleet. (Bombardier/Canadair)

An Amakusa Airlines de Havilland Canada DHC-8-100. (Amakusa Airlines)

Japan Airlines took delivery of the Boeing 777-200ER. (Jeffhuang0627, Wikimedia Commons Licence Creative Commons Attribution-Share Alike 4.0 International https://commons.wikimedia. org/wiki/File:JA704J_Japan_Airlines_ Boeing_777-246(ER)_Clear_to_Take_off_ from_TSA_RW10.jpg)

The Boeing 767-300ER also joined the JAL fleet. (Kentaro Lemoto, Creative Commons Licence CC BY-SA 2.0 https://commons.wikimedia.org/wiki/Category:JA655J_(aircraft)#/media/File:JAL_B767-300ER(JA655J)_(6317678835).jpg)

Right: The economy class cabin in a Boeing 777-200ER (Hideyuki KAMON, Creative Commons Licence CC BY-SA 2.0 https://commons.wikimedia.org/wiki/Category:Japan_Airlines_aircraft_cabins#/media/File:Japan_Airlines_777-200ER_Economy_cabin.jpg)

Below: Boeing 747-400 JA8908 seen in the Walt Disney 'Friends' livery. (contri, Creative Commons Licence CC BY-SA 2.0 https://commons.wikimedia.org/wiki/Category:JA8908_(aircraft)#/media/File:Japan_Airlines_Boeing_747-446D_(JA8908-26352-978)_(13486345385).jpg)

Above: Boeing 747-400 in the Walt Disney 'Sweet' livery. (Steven Byles, Creative Commons Licence VV BY-SA 2.0 https://commons.wikimedia.org/wiki/Category:JAL_Dream_Express?uselang=ja#/media/File:JAL_B747-446D_JA8904_JAL50th_(5315271258).jpg)

Left: Nose detail of JA8904 'Sweet'. (Jozef Mols collection)

JA8905 was painted into the Tokyo DisneySea livery. (Jozef Mols collection)

Chapter 8

The Merger

During the first years of the new millennium, the Japanese aviation industry experienced major problems. A worldwide economic downturn resulted in lower passenger numbers, while the 9/11 terrorist attacks in New York and the SARS pandemic in 2003 further impacted the sector. JAL's competitor Hokkaido International Airlines (Air Do) had to enter Japanese corporate restructuring procedures after the Hokkaido prefectural government, which had already injected large amounts of money into the carrier, refused to invest further in the airline.[1]

JAL and JAS also encountered difficulties. In 2001, domestic passenger market share was 25.3 per cent for JAL and 23.8 per cent for JAS, competing directly on 33 routes. Together with the third Japanese carrier, ANA, the three major companies accounted for 97.8 per cent of the domestic market.[2] In November 2001, JAL and JAS announced the start of talks on a potential merger between the two carriers, with the intent to create the world's sixth largest airline in terms of passenger miles. The move would leave the domestic airline market dominated by only two groups, All Nippon Airways with a group share of 49 per cent, and JAL-JAS with 48 per cent.[3] A possible merger would be the first major realignment in Japan's airline market in three decades and was announced some weeks after the collapse of several other airlines around the globe, including Swissair, Sabena and Ansett Australia. Together, JAS and JAL operated 257 aircraft and employed more than 52,000 people, generating a net revenue of $17.4bn (£13.6bn).[4] For JAL, already the fourth largest foreign carrier in terms of capacity after Air France, British Airways and Lufthansa, the merger would mean an improved standing among the world's global commercial airlines and a stronger domestic base for its high-yield international operations. For JAS, the merger would relieve economic and competitive pressure in the Japanese domestic network. Naturally, both airlines hoped to reduce overall costs. For ANA, however, this merger would cause serious problems; when JAL and JAS announced their merger negotiations, ANA informed its shareholders that it was expecting a $90m loss for the year ending March 2002[5]. JAL and JAS, on the other hand, announced that the merger would allow them to cut 73bn yen (£370m) by fiscal year 2005, but with the simultaneous shedding of 3,000 workers and a decision to share aircraft and facilities.[6]

ANA duly challenged the merger proposal and filed a petition with the Fair Trade Commission against it, claiming that the merger would cause the current market structure to become anti-competitive, not to mention adversely affecting passenger convenience.[7] As it turned out, the Fair Trade Commission had some doubts of its own about the merger, believing that the creation of a duopoly in the domestic market would reduce fare competition on key routes in a sector that already suffered from insufficient competition.[8] In the capital-intense and highly competitive air industry, any new airlines would face a serious challenge to get off the ground, as a JAL-JAS combination would be in possession of most slots at Japan's congested airports. Additionally, airlines around the world had a history of temporarily lowering prices to ward off upstart airlines and then raising them again later. A JAL-JAS combination would have the power to settle prices in Japan on its own.[9] In its findings, the Fair Trade Commission focused on the domestic passenger transport business area, especially for travel to and from Haneda airport in Tokyo and Itami airport (Osaka), taking into account the routes operated by JAL and JAS concurrently. The examination did not focus on the areas of international air passenger transport, international air cargo or domestic air cargo, since more than one powerful competing air carrier existed.[10]

In view of the remarks from the Fair Trade Commission, JAL and JAS responded with some remedial measures in April 2002. Under the revised proposals, JAL and JAS agreed to provide facilities for new entrants, including boarding bridges and gate ports at Haneda airport and other airports on request. They would also return nine turnaround (or 18 single) slots at Haneda airport for the use of new entrants.[11] As a result, the Fair Trade Commission decided that the proposed merger was unlikely to breach Article 10 of the Antimonopoly Act and gave it the green light.[12] In October 2002, JAL and JAS established a new holding company called Japan Airlines System, forming the new core of the JAL group. In so doing, the new company inherited JAS's entire fleet, mainly composed of Airbus A300s and Boeing 777s plus McDonnell Douglas MD-80 and MD-90 aircraft. An integrated timetable was also prepared. All of JAS's subsidiaries, including Japan Air Commuter and Hokkaido Air System, were part of the merger. In 2002, two of the JAS Airbus aircraft were scrapped at Sendai airport and two others were transferred to Fly Air in Turkey.[13] On 1 April 2004, the 'old' Japan Airlines changed its name to Japan Airlines International and JAS changed its name to Japan Airlines Domestic, thus officially ending the JAS brand.[14] JAS flight codes were changed to JAL flight codes, while JAS check-in desks were amended to JAL livery and JAS aircraft were gradually repainted. On 23 June 2004, the parent company Japan Airlines System was renamed to Japan Airlines Corporation. On 1 October 2006, Japan Airlines International and Japan Airlines Domestic merged into a single brand, Japan Airlines International.[15] Before this merger, both airlines had integrated their personnel and wage systems. The integration of IT systems cost about 500m yen (£2.5m).[16]

Shortly after the merger, JAL started up a route between Fukuoka and Shanghai, using a Boeing 767. In 2004, the airline opened a new route between Tokyo and Hengzhou at the same time as ANA. In 2007, flights from Tokyo to Shanghai followed. In 2005, JAL ordered a total of 40 Boeing 737-800 aircraft, the first of which was delivered a year later. The new jets would mainly be used by JEX.[17] Although not a direct result of problems with the former JAS McDonnell Douglas aircraft, the arrival of the Boeings solved some of the airline's problems, since JAS had had to ground all of its DC-9-81s and 87s due to engine cracks.[18] In the meantime, Harlequin Air, which had been owned by JAL Domestic, ceased operations in April 2005 due to the restructuring of the JAL group.[19] J-Air, which had introduced the Bombardier CR200, saw little opportunity for route expansion of its own from its home at Hiroshima-Nishi airport. After the opening of the Chubu Centrair International Airport, however, J-Air realised its dream and relocated to its new home at Nagoya airfield. In order to strengthen the recognition of the JAL brand and improve customer convenience, the airline discarded its own flight numbers and changed to JAL flight numbers from April 2005.[20]

If one looks at the immediate results of the JAL-JAS merger, it is interesting to note that the holding company, Japan Airlines Systems, slashed its profit outlook. In March 2003, it announced that a group operating profit of $17m (£13.2m) was expected after a JAL/JAS operating loss of 1bn yen (£5m) in 2002. According to Japan Airlines Systems, the low profit was a result of customers worried about the situation in Iraq. Furthermore, the Bali bombing and a typhoon in Guam had depressed demand. At the same time, the airline said it planned to cut an additional 600 jobs, or 2.8 per cent of its workforce by March 2006, on top of the already announced 3,000 staff reductions.[21] Passengers, in the meantime, faced a rise in airfares on domestic flights of about 1.2 per cent, which was negligible if one compares the rise with the general level of inflation.

Above: Before the merger with JAL, this Airbus A300-600 was part of the JAS fleet. It was integrated ino the JAL fleet in 2004. (Jozef Mols collection)

Right: JAS also used Boeing 777 aircraft, which were integrated into JAL's fleet following the merger. (Amayagan, commons wikimedia, CCO licence (public domain) https://commons.wikimedia.org/wiki/Category:Boeing_777-200_of_Japan_Air_System#/media/File:JapanAirSystem_B777-200_fukuoka_20050213151538.jpg)

A JAS Boeing 777 with the small JAL logo already on the fuselage following the merger. (Amayagan, commons wikimedia, CCO licence public domain https://commons.wikimedia.org/wiki/Category:JA007D_(aircraft)#/media/File:JAS-Boeing_777-289-JA007D-Fukuoka_airport-20050213-141646.JPG)

Above: Following the merger, several McDonnell Douglas aircraft were integrated into the JAL fleet, but many of them had to be grounded due to cracks in the engines. (contri, wikimedia commons CC BY-SA 2.0 https://commons.wikimedia.org/wiki/Category:JA8279_(aircraft)#/media/File:Japan_Air_System_McDonnell_Douglas_MD-87_(JA8279-49465-1604)_-_Flickr_-_contri.jpg)

Left: JAC Japan Air Commuter, an affiliate of JAS, was also absorbed into the JAL-JAS group after the merger. (Jozef Mols collection)

This JAC Japan Air Commuter Saab 340 received JAL livery following the merger of parent company JAS with JAL. (lasta29, Wikimedia Commons licence CC BY 2.0 https://commons.wikimedia.org/wiki/Category:JA8594_(aircraft)#/media/File:Japan_Air_Commuter,_Saab_340B,_JA8594_(17165703268).jpg)

Japan Air Commuter also used the de Havilland DHC-8-400, examples of which were taken over by JAL following the merger between parent company JAC and JAL. (Amayagan, wikimedia commons licence CC0 Public Domain, https://commons.wikimedia.org/wiki/Category:JA841C_(aircraft)#/media/File:JapanAirCommuter_DHC-8-400_fukuoka_20040911141328.jpg)

Hokkaido Air System, an affiliate of JAS, was also integrated into the JAS-JAL group following the merger. This Saab 340 was therefore also transferred to the JAL fleet. (Japanbird, wikimedia commons licence CC BY-SA 4.0 https://commons.wikimedia.org/wiki/Category:JA02HC_(aircraft)#/media/File:HAC_JA02HC_20180813.jpg)

JAL ordered Boeing 737-800s, most of which were used by Japan Air Express (JEX). (lasta29, wikimedia commons licence CC BY 2.0 https://commons.wikimedia.org/wiki/Category:JAL_Express#/media/File:Japan_Air_Lines,_B_737-800,_JA347J_(23557730273).jpg)

Harlequin Air was also fully integrated into the JAL group. (Amayagan, wikimedia commons licence Amayagan CC0 public domain, https://commons.wikimedia.org/wiki/Category:JA8552_(aircraft)#/media/File:HarlequinAir_MD-81_fukuoka_20041023120134.jpg)

The Arc of the Sun

While JAL and JAS were finalising their merger, the airline group decided it was time to change the company livery used on its fleet. The previous livery, called the 'tsurumaru' or 'crane circle', was designed in 1958 by Jerry Huff, the creative director at Botsford, Constantine and Gardner of San Francisco. Inspired by the personal crests of Samurai families, Huff designed a logo of a Japanese red-crown crane with its wings extended in full flight. The tsurumaru livery would be used until 2002, when it began to be replaced by the 'Arc of the Sun' livery. Designed by brand-identity firm Landor Associates, this featured the motif of a rising sun on a creamy parchment-coloured background.[1,2] Rebranding began in April 2002 and was completed in April 2004. Landor Associates designed 300,000 specific items for JAL,[3] including not only the logo on the aircraft tail, but also in-flight equipment and other visual images. By 2007, the Arc of the Sun livery would go on to be adopted by other airlines within the JAL group.

Although very costly to implement, a change of logo does not immediately attract new clients. Therefore, JAL also decided to increase passenger comfort on board its long-distance aircraft. The new 'Skysleeper Solo' seat, based on human engineering theory and designed to make long flights more comfortable, was introduced in 2001 in the First Class cabins of Tokyo to New York flights. In 2002, JAL was awarded 'Airline of the Year for 2002' by *Air Transport* magazine for unremitting effort towards structural reform. The same year, the new 'JAL Shell Flat Seat' was introduced on the executive class 'Seasons' service between Tokyo and London. Additionally, in order to simplify flight boarding procedures, the first automatic check-in machine on an international route in Japan began operation at Narita airport.

In the meantime, JAL also opened a new route between Tokyo and Hanoi through a code-sharing agreement with Vietnam Airlines.

On 31 October 2005, JAL retired its last McDonnell Douglas DC-10. As part of the JAL Medium Term Corporate Plan for 2005–07, the airline also announced that it would retire its oldest Boeing 747 aircraft. The last Boeing 747-300 would fly from Honolulu to Tokyo on 30 July 2009, after 26 years of service with the airline. Shortly afterwards, JAL terminated the assignments of 130 American contract 747 pilots based in Hawaii and closed its Oahu office. In 2006, with the 2006 FIFA World Cup kicking off in Germany, JAL showed support for the Japanese national football team by painting aircraft in a special design entitled 'Samurai Blue 2006'. On international flights, the livery was displayed on a Boeing 777-300, operating on Japan Airlines' daily non-stop service from Narita to Frankfurt, and on a Boeing 747-400 operating other international routes. Another Boeing 777, used on domestic services also received the livery. JAL had already been an official supporting company of the national team since 1999, providing transportation assistance to team members and officials.

2006 also saw JAL unveil its 'JAL Tamagotchi Jet' special livery in support of the sales of Tamagotchi toys. Tamagotchi is a brand of handheld digital pets that was created in Japan by Akihiro Yokoi of WiZ and Aki Maiti of Bandai. It was released by Bandai on 23 November 1996 in Japan and in the United States on 1 May 1997, quickly becoming one of the biggest toy fads of the late 1990s and the early 2000s. As of June 2023, more than 91 million units have been sold worldwide. Most Tamagotchi are housed in a small egg-shaped handheld video game with an interface consisting of three buttons, with the Tamagotchi Pix adding a shutter on the top to activate the camera. When JAL launched this paint scheme, Tamagotchi had just introduced the 'Jalchi' toy plane on its video games.

Another special livery had the words 'Let's stop global warming' painted on the fuselage of a Boeing 777. JAL indicated during the presentation of this livery that, for example, a Boeing 777-200 flying from Haneda to Sapporo would use about 19,700 litres of fuel or the equivalent of about 330 cars with full tanks. The airline explained that the Japanese transportation sector, including cars, buses, cargo vehicles and aircraft made up about 20 per cent of CO_2 emissions. Air transportation accounted for about four per cent of this, or about 0.8 per cent of total emissions in Japan. In 2008, JAL would paint two of its 777s in 'Eco Jet'-livery.

Amid all this, the airline had decided that joining a global aviation alliance was the ideal way forward. On 1 April 2007, JAL, together with four sister airlines, became an affiliate member of Oneworld. This was the alliance's biggest expansion in its young history, Malev and Royal Jordanian also joined the alliance on that day.[4] Shortly afterwards, the first JAL aircraft with a special Oneworld design entered service. A few months later, Japan Asia Airways and JAL International merged as JAL received authorisation to operate its own flights between Japan and Taiwan. This integration of Japan Asia Airways would result in further cost cuts.[5] Japan Asia Airways would fly for the last time on the Taipei–Nagoya route on 31 March 2008, concluding 32 years of operations; services to Taiwan were transferred to JAL the following day. Immediately afterwards, JAL signed a purchase agreement with Embraer for ten Embraer 170 jets, with options to acquire another five aircraft. The contract value was worth approximately $435m (£340m) if all options were exercised. The aircraft would be used for linking tier-two and tier-three cities in Japan, to bypass the airline's congested hub in Tokyo. Configured to seat 76 passengers in a single-class layout, they were operated by J-Air, the first examples being delivered in October 2008.[6]

While the JAL-JAS group was working on its integration of operations and fleets, JAL decided to participate in the creation of a new airline outside the group. Galaxy Airlines was established as a domestic cargo airline by Sagawa Express (90 per cent) and JAL (10 per cent). The airline started operations from Tokyo International Airport in 2006 with flights from Tokyo to Naha airport in Okinawa and New Kitakyushu airport in Kyushu. Two Airbus A300-600F freighters were operated. Later on, Osaka and Hokkaido were added to the flight schedule, but the airline closed down in 2008.[7] In 2009, JAL Express started operating international flights, linking Kansai Osaka International Airport with Hangzhou in China.

JAL also had to face competition. Skymark Airlines was now operating under court protection, but remained a competitor nevertheless. ANA countered the JAL-JAS group by expanding its own, mainly domestic network through the establishment of new subsidiaries and co-operation with new entrants into the market. Ibex Airlines was established in 1999 and started operations on 7 August 2000 between Sendai and Osaka, under the name of Fair Inc. It reached a co-operation agreement with ANA, under which it provided assistance in several capacities, including flight operations, flight crew provision, maintenance and engineering services. Later on, in 2002, the airline began services at Tokyo's Narita International Airport. In 2004, Fair Inc changed its name to Ibex Airlines and started to use the ANA Connection logo.[8] In August 2004, ANA established Air Next Co Ltd as a wholly owned low-cost subsidiary based at Fukuoka airport. The airline operated domestic services with a fleet of Boeing 737-500s. Subsequently, Air Next, Air Central and Air Nippon Network were merged and rebranded as ANA Wings.[9]

In 2002, Kobe Airlines was established as a 'hybrid airline', providing a higher level of service than the low-cost airlines, while its operating costs were lower than full-service airlines. In May 2003, the airline changed its name to Starflyer. The company had been formed by a former Japan Airlines technician, Takaaki Hon, and a former All Nippon Airways executive by the name of Yasushi Muto. ANA began an operational relationship with StarFlyer in 2005, allowing StarFlyer to use its computerised reservations system. This relationship expanded to code-sharing in 2007, under which StarFlyer services between Haneda and Kitakyushu and Fukuoka were marketed under ANA's airline code. In 2008, StarFlyer commenced charter flights to Seoul and prepared to start up regular services at a future date. In addition, it was also planning charter flights to Hong Kong and packaged tour charters from Kitakyushu to Guam. Following the 2011 Tohoku earthquake and tsunami and the consequent massive cancellation of flights, ANA announced that it had acquired an 18 per cent stake in StarFlyer, making it the largest shareholder.[10]

A Boeing 767-300 in the new 'Arc of the Sun' livery. (Kentaro Lemoto, CC BY-SA 2.0, https://commons.wikimedia.org/wiki/Category:JA8265_(aircraft)?uselang=ja#/media/File:JAL_B767-300(JA8265)_(5066915245).jpg)

In 2003, besides the 'Arc of the Sun' livery, some Boeing 767-300s received the 'Yokoso! Japan' logo, part of a Visit Japan campaign promoted by the Ministry of Land, Infrastructure, Transport and Tourism. (Amayagan, wikimedia commons licence CCO public domain – https://commons.wikimedia.org/wiki/Category:JA8266_(aircraft)?uselang=ja#/media/File:JapanAirlines_B767-300_fukuoka_20041227133800.jpg)

Top: This Boeing 747-400 was also painted with the 'Yokoso! Japan' logo. (Kentaro Lemoto, Creative Commons Attribution-Share Alike 2.0 Generic license. https://commons.wikimedia.org/wiki/File:JAL_B747-400(JA8916)_(4184195679).jpg)

Above: Former JAS aircraft, like this Airbus A300-B4, also received the new Arc of the Sun livery. (Jozef Mols collection)

Right: JAL McDonnell Douglas MD-87 in the new livery. (Jozef Mols collection)

Even the smaller aircraft of the JAL fleet, like this Saab 340, received the 'Arc of the Sun livery. (Jozef Mols collection)

Left: **When JAL joined the One World alliance, many of its aircraft received a special logo, including this Boeing 777-200. (Kentaro Lemoto, Creative Commons Attribution-Share Alike 2.0 Generic license. https://commons.wikimedia.org/wiki/File:JAL_B777-200(JA771J)_(6907607110).jpg)**

Below: **This Boeing 777-300 received a different One World livery. (One World)**

For J-Air, JAL ordered a series of Embraer 170 jets. (lasta29, CC BY 2.0 https://fr.wikipedia.org/wiki/J-Air#/media/Fichier:J-Air,_ERJ-170,_JA225J_(21740434669).jpg)

Right: In 2008, JAL put into service this Boeing 767-300 with a special livery to support Tokyo's bid for the 2016 Olympic and Paralympic Games. (Amayagan, Creative Commons Licence CC0 public domain, https://commons.wikimedia.org/wiki/Category:JA8364_(aircraft)#/media/File:JapanAirlines_B767-300_fukuoka_20081212132904.jpg)

Below: This Boeing 777-300 received the special 'Samurai Blue' livery in support of the Japanese national football team. (Jozef Mols collection)

Above: In 2006, JAL launched the 'Tamagotchi' livery on its Boeing 777. (Jozef Mols collection)

Left: The Boeing 777 with 'Let's stop global warming' on the fuselage. (Jozef Mols collection)

Below: To further underline the importance JAL gives to the protection of the environment, two Boeing 777s received the special 'Eco Jet' logo. (Kentaro Lemoto, CC BY-SA 2.0 https://commons.wikimedia.org/wiki/Category:JA8984_(aircraft)#/media/File:JAL_B777-200(JA8984)_(4852687087).jpg)

Right: New Sky Suite economy cabin. (JAL)

Below: Ibex Airlines provided feeder services for ANA from regional airports with a fleet of Bombardier CRJ 700 jets. (Alan Wilson, CC BY-SA 2.0https://en.wikipedia.org/wiki/Ibex_Airlines#/media/File:Bombardier_CRJ-702_%E2%80%98JA09RJ%E2%80%99_IBEX_Airlines_(47001512774).jpg)

Bottom: Competitor Starflyer used the Airbus A320-200. (Alec Wilson, CC BY SA 2.0 https://en.wikipedia.org/wiki/StarFlyer#/media/File:JA23MC_(29890762650).jpg)

Chapter 10

Bankrupt

Although JAL was still the largest Asian carrier in terms of revenue, the airline suffered steep financial losses. Some of its problems were related to dwindling reservations due to the worldwide economic crisis following the Gulf War (which caused fuel prices to rise), the swine flu pandemic and the Lehman Brothers bankruptcy in 2008.[1] Between 2006 and 2009, the number of passengers decreased from 58m to 52.9m.[2] As revenue dropped, JAL began to encounter cashflow problems. In the case of the airline industry, operating costs are mostly fixed, consisting of wages, aircraft lease payments, fuel and maintenance costs. JAL had excessive fixed costs while its income steadily declined during the economic crisis,[3] so planned job cuts equal to ten per cent of the total work force, which at the end of April 2009 stood at 49,830. The airline simultaneously intended to scrap some 20 of its international flights by March 2012, resulting in a 20 per cent drop in sales from overseas flights. On the other hand, the airline obtained a 100bn yen (£534m) government-backed credit line, followed a few months later by a second guarantee of the same amount.[4]

Though cancelling some loss-making flights might have helped JAL to solve its immediate problems, there were more institutional issues that needed a remedy. The company had too many aircraft, too many personnel and too many routes. The flight routes were not the direct drivers of fixed costs, so eliminating the unprofitable routes alone would not alleviate JAL's situation. Instead, it was the planes and personnel that constituted the more severe issues. Due to Narita airport's imposition of limits on the share of slots, JAL, with its focus on international business, chose to compensate by operating large aircraft such as the Boeing 747. These planes, however, became uncompetitive assets as the industry standard moved towards more efficient smaller aircraft. As for personnel, JAL had a workforce of nearly 50,000 workers, which was considered at least 30 per cent too many. Therefore, cuts of ten per cent, as JAL intended, would not be enough to solve the problem. JAL had been known for its aggressive recruitment strategy in the past but, in 1975, decided to decrease the number of new hires, as the industry was becoming more competitive. However, this caused a 'reversed pyramid' effect in the company's human resource structure, with too many veterans and too few young employees. Even after the merger with JAS, JAL continued to pay as much as 500,000 yen (£2,675) a month to some retired office employees, while young employees only received 200,000 yen (£1,070).[5] As for financial liabilities, JAL had bloated bank loans, but also pension liabilities and losses from fuel-related derivatives that aimed to compensate for business losses. By the end of the fall of 2009, JAL had negative assets of more than 800bn yen (£4.2bn), close to the amount of financial liabilities.[6]

Other OneWorld partners that wanted to safeguard their Asian interests tried to come up with solutions. Air France-KLM, members of competing Skyteam, started up talks with JAL to form an alliance in which the European company would inject a few hundred million dollars and take a minority share in the struggling carrier.[7] British Airways, on the other hand, made it clear that it was trying to help money-losing JAL in order to prevent the airline from being lured away from its OneWorld alliance. Although British Airways had been in talks with JAL for many months, negotiations focused on co-operation, rather than on any cash bailout. At a time when JAL reported its biggest-ever quarterly loss of $1bn (£785m) in the three months ending in June 2009, it was reported that American Airlines and Qantas Airways had also offered a 'broad financial and business support' to their ailing partner, including a possible investment of several hundred million dollars from American.[8] The proposal was aimed at thwarting Delta Air Lines, another member of the rival SkyTeam alliance, which was also in talks with JAL. Rumours, mainly in the press, had indeed suggested that JAL would prefer to reject American Airlines's proposal (and the Oneworld alliance) and 'defect' to the SkyTeam alliance, joining Delta Air Lines. Delta and JAL covered many of the same routes, allowing the two airlines better efficiency through schedule and fare collaboration.[9, 10] JAL nevertheless said in a statement that media reports of a tie-up with a foreign carrier were not based on official information from the company and that nothing had been decided.[11]

While talks were ongoing it became clear that only a few options remained open for struggling JAL. The airline submitted a restructuring plan under which it pledged to cut operating costs by 30 per cent through various measures, including cutting 6,800 jobs or roughly 14 per cent of its workforce, as well as eliminating 50 routes. Transport minister Seiji Maehara argued that the cost-cutting measures did not go far enough. Some creditors suggested a more drastic idea of splitting the airline into 'good' and 'bad' parts, as American automaker General Motors had done, but analysts had doubts that this technique could apply to airlines. 'Air carriers use the same aircraft and workforce in the whole network. It will be impossible to separate them', it was said.[12] With 'Open Sky' deregulation proceeding worldwide, the transport minister argued that JAL's restructuring should be seen in the broader context of how to bolster Japan's airline industry. In the USA, Northwest had been bought by Delta Air Lines while in Europe, Air France had merged with KLM. Was the same scenario possible in Japan? Would it be feasable to separate out JAL's international operations and merge them with ANA? Under such a scenario, JAL would become a local airline focusing on domestic and short-haul international flights. An alliance with a viable foreign partner was also an option, to help JAL weed out unprofitable routes and lower its operating costs. Unlike the previous government, which had welcomed talks, the new transport minister was not enthusiastic about such an idea. If, however, a deal with a foreign carrier did prove necessary, American Airlines would be the preferred partner. The logic of having Delta support JAL had been questioned, given that Delta and Northwest Airlines (which Delta had acquired) had been through bankruptcy proceedings themselves. Others, including Himeno of Mitsubishi UFJ Securities, said that a bankruptcy, although a 'worst case scenario', would not be bad for JAL, as it would mean the airline could cut legacy costs with the unions without their approval.[13]

The scenario of a bankruptcy was nonetheless opposed by JAL's boss, President and CEO Haruko Nishimatsu. According to him, the airline would have a better chance of tapping future growth in the Asian market by switching its carrier alliance. That would mean forming a partnership with Delta Air Lines rather than American Airlines, and as a result shifting to the Delta-led SkyTeam group. A bankruptcy would lead to a drop in customer confidence, given the 'bankruptcy image', according to Nishimatsu. His remarks made it clear that JAL was opposed to a court-backed deal, suggesting that the carrier's last-minute negotiations would continue with a turnaround fund until an aid package was formulated later on. At the same time, Nishimatsu indicated that he was willing to reduce the scale of international operations by switching to more fuel-efficient smaller aircraft, while maintaining the airline's overseas network as much as possible.[14]

In the end, JAL saw no other solution but to follow the proposals from the government-backed turn-around council, and on 19 January 2010, filed for protection from its creditors. Routes were slashed and the workforce was further reduced in a move to rebuild the balance sheet, and Kazuo Inamori was appointed as chairman of the airline. In return for a massive injection of public money, JAL was prohibited from freely expanding its route network, being obliged to boost its earnings capacity on existing routes.[15] As a result, Japan Airlines and its partner airline American Airlines decided to strengthen their partnership and apply for approval of American anti-trust immunity on trans-Pacific routes. This would allow JAL to adjust its networks, flight schedules and other business activities.[16]

In the meantime, a government-backed turnaround body had made final arrangements to use around 700bn yen (£3.75bn) in public funds for loans and investments to rehabilitate Japan Airlines through court-backed bankruptcy proceedings. The Enterprise Turnaround Initiative Corp (ETIC) of Japan, funded by both the government and private financial institutions, planned to create a credit line of 400bn yen (£2.14bn) and invest about 300bn yen (£1.6bn) in Japan's top carrier. At the same time, the entity asked JAL's main creditor banks to waive 300bn yen (£1.6bn) in debt. In exchange, the entity asked JAL to cut more than 10,000 jobs. Furthermore, ETIC aimed to improve JAL's asset holdings by dissolving excessive liabilities through drawing down and then replenishing capital, as well as through the elimination of nearly 70bn yen (£374m) in corporate bonds. At the same time, ETIC planned to set aside a pool of around 400bn yen (£2.14bn) in loans to avoid cash shortages and to finance business transactions for purchasing fuel, aircraft parts and other items necessary to maintain key operations.[17] JAL's shares were de-listed from the Japanese Stock Exchange.

Under the control of ETIC, JAL reduced its fleet from 279 aircraft in 2009 to 215 aircraft in 2012, and all Boeing 747s left the fleet. At the same time, the number of destinations on its timetable was reduced by 30 per cent and a total of 18,000 workers had to leave the company.[18] The rumours, and later confirmation of bankruptcy hit JAL, but also undermined confidence in other Japanese airlines. Domestic travel on JAL and ANA combined was down some ten per cent (compared to 2008) as a combined result of the economic downturn worldwide and the JAL bankruptcy. However, by May 2010, both ANA and JAL could announce total passenger traffic was up by 7.8 per cent on a year-on-year basis. More surprisingly, JAL, which was under pressure to downsize and axe unprofitable routes, had seen its passenger numbers rise by 1.1 per cent, although ANA's load factor on domestic routes (63.5 per cent) was still higher than JAL's 59.9 per cent. On international routes, JAL managed a load factor of 70.8 per cent, compared to 76.6 per cent for ANA.[19]

In March 2011, JAL emerged from court-administered bankruptcy after slashing 16,000 jobs cutting pension benefits and closing parts of its international and domestic networks. The bail-out body, which pledged in 2009 to sell the shares it had obtained during the restructuring period, started the process of picking underwriters for the JAL stake it would sell.[20] In July 2011, ETIC selected Nomura Holdings, Daiwa Securities, Mitsubishi UFJ, Morgan Stanley, Mizuho Securities, SMBC and Nikko Securities to underwrite the sale of its equity stake without specifying amounts or dates. On 6 January 2012, JAL announced its intention to relist its shares on the Tokyo Stock Exchange in an initial public offering of up to 1tn yen (£5.3bn). The ETIC sold its entire holding in JAL for 650bn yen (£3.5bn) or nearly double its investment in 2010. Following its exit from bankruptcy protection, JAL could begin several new partnerships with the Oneworld alliance and its partners. The trans-Pacific co-operation with American, for example, started in April 2011.[21]

Chapter 11

A New Start

JAL's exit from bankruptcy in March 2011 did not mean that all of its problems were solved; the airline still had to fight to consolidate its market position. The airline had to adopt a new corporate policy, so announced its intention to change its logo from 1 April 2011, symbolising a fresh start. The high-flying crane from the Tsurumaru livery, symbol of the airline for many years, made its return to JAL aircraft tails. Staff uniforms remained the same, but all other items such as stationery, name tags and so on would be phased out over the next years. JAL's official trademarked name was changed from Japan Airlines International Co Ltd to Japan Airlines Co Ltd.[1]

More important than external symbols were the steps taken by the airline to set up cost-cutting co-operation with other global airlines. On 12 May 2011, Reuters reported that British Airways and JAL had agreed on a revenue-sharing deal for flights between Europe and Japan, potentially giving their Oneworld alliance more competitive muscle.[2] Shortly afterwards, Finnair announced that it was seeking to join a British Airways-JAL business arrangement to co-ordinate schedules and share revenue on flights to Japan, as Finnair expanded ties with the Oneworld alliance members. Japan was one of Finnair's core markets and the airline was looking forward to the benefits of a strategic joint business agreement. Finnair, British Airways and JAL between them operated ten routes between Europe and Japan at that time, with JAL providing the majority of services linking Tokyo to London, Paris, Frankfurt and Helsinki.[3] In the meantime, JAL and American Airlines had also announced the commencement of their joint business on trans-Pacific routes from 1 April, 2011.[4] Finnair then announced it would partner in a trans-Atlantic business joint venture with American airlines and British Airways.[5]

JAL's management also decided to make changes to the fleet in order to operate more efficiently and cut costs. The last Airbus A300 (obtained through the merger with JAS) left the fleet on 31 May 2011, while the last McDonnell Douglas MD90 was retired after its last flight from Hiroshima to Haneda on 30 March 2013. In order to replace the sold Boeing 747s, the airline ordered the Boeing 787 Dreamliner. In May 2012, a Boeing 777-200, JA772J, received the 'Gambare! Nippon' ('Go for it, Japan') livery in support of Team Japan in the 2012 Summer Olympic Games to be held in London. By the end of the year, JAL had treated JA773J to a livery supporting Tokyo's bid for the 2020 Summer Olympic Games, using this aircraft on domestic routes. JAL also promoted other Japanese products or companies by offering them special liveries, such as those for the Samantha Thavasa luxury fashion house and the Arashi boys band.

Another major decision was made in 2012, when JAL launched a low-cost airline, headquartered in Narita with a second base to be opened later in Osaka. Jetstar Japan Co was a joint venture with Qantas (33.3 per cent), JAL (33.3 per cent), Mitsubishi Corporation (16.7 per cent) and Century Leasing Corporation (16.7 per cent). The original capital was 12bn yen (£63.5m), but when Qantas and Japan Airlines each injected further capital, these two airlines each obtained 45.7 per cent of the shares. Its first services linked Narita with Fukuoka, Okinawa, Osaka and Sapporo. The airline's CEO, Miyuki Suzuki, indicated that Jetstar Japan's network strategy would be focused on the domestic market from Narita, and that the company would try to optimise its schedule for connecting traffic with international flights operated by Australian-based Jetstar Airways. In 2014, the airline announced the establishment of code-share and frequent-flyer programme agreements with parent airline Japan Airlines. This gave the airline a distinction from traditional low-cost carriers such as Peach and Vanilla Air, which were both affiliated with All Nippon Airways but lacked similar agreements with ANA. For its operations, the airline used a fleet of Airbus A320-family jets.[6] A few years later, Jetstar started flights to Hong Kong and Taipei. In 2014, American Airlines, already a JAL partner, announced a code-share agreement with Jetstar, which would enhance American's network across Japan.

Although JAL had only been resurrected a few years, new decisions surprised analysts. The carrier had just ordered Boeing 787 jets, but now signed a deal with Airbus with an order of 31 Airbus A350 jets (with an option for 25 more), making an investment of $9.5bn (£7.4bn), with deliveries expected by 2014. The decision was made after the carrier had experienced many problems with the Boeing 787 jets. First of all, deliveries had been delayed many times, and 787s had been grounded worldwide because of problems with the batteries. This deal was historic as JAL had always been a faithful Boeing client.[7]

Another major surprise came when JAL and the Mitsubishi Aircraft Corporation announced in 2014 that the carrier had reached a basic agreement with the manufacturer to purchase 32 Mitsubishi Regional Jets (MRJ) as the next-generation regional jet for its fleet. It was the intention to deploy the new aircraft on domestic routes, starting in 2021. This would have been the first time JAL owned a Japanese-built passenger aircraft since the former JAS Group operated the YS-11. Unfortunately, Mitsubishi subsequently had to shelve its project due to competition. At the same time, JAL also indicated it had ordered 15 Embraer E-jets, comprising additional E-170s and new orders for the E-190, together with an additional 12 options for the two jets.[8] As well as ordering new aircraft, the airline refurbished the cabins of existing jets. In 2013, JAL debuted new versions of its economy and premium economy seats called Sky Premium and Sky Wider Economy respectively. The Sky Premium seats, found on selected 777-300s and soon 787s, featured the same width as the Sky Shell seats but with a 4in larger seat pitch of 42 inches and a 3in greater recline of up to 10in compared to a 39in pitch and 7in recline on the Sky Shell. The Sky Wider Economy seats found on select 767s and select 777-300s feature slimmer seats with 4in more legroom and another inch of width plus a larger PTV screen. In premium cabins, JAL introduced fully lie-flat seats, branded as Sky Suite in Business Class cabins, and enhanced First Seat seats in First Class cabins.[9] The JAL Sky Suite was named Best Business Class Airline Seat at the SKYTRAX 2013 World Airline Awards.

This Boeing 777 received a special 'Tokyo 2020' livery to support Japan's bid to host the Olympic Games in 2020. (wikimedia commons, CC BY-SA 4.0 https://commons.wikimedia.org/wiki/Category:JA773J_(aircraft)#/media/ File:JAL_JA773J.jpg)

Above: The Samantha Thavasa livery promoted a Japanese luxury fashion house. (wikimedia.commons, Kentaro Lemoto, Creative Commons Attribution-Share Alike 2.0 Generic https://commons.wikimedia.org/wiki/File:JAL_B777-200%28JA8983%29_%285478939174%29.jpg)

Right: JAL also promoted Arashi boy band with this special livery. (wikimedia.commons., Kentaro Lemoto, CC BY-SA 2.0 https://commons.wikimedia.org/wiki/Category:JA8982_(aircraft)#/media/File:JAL_B777-200(JA8982)_(5025480623).jpg)

A Jetstar Japan Airbus A320-200. (Alan Wilson, CC BY-SA 2.0 https://en.wikipedia.org/wiki/Jetstar_Japan#/media/File:Airbus_A320-232_%E2%80%98JA03JJ%E2%80%99_Jetstar_Japan_(48607602916).jpg)

First Class suite on a Boeing 777-300ER. (public domain, https://commons.wikimedia.org/wiki/Category:Japan_Airlines_aircraft_cabins#/media/File:JAL_First_Class_Suite_777-300ER.JPG)

Left: The First Class suite was revealed shortly after JAL re-emerged from bankruptcy. (EIHEITAI-EISHI Public Domain https://commons.wikimedia.org/wiki/Category:Japan_Airlines_aircraft_cabins#/media/File:JAL_International_flight_F-class_seat_%22SUITE%222.JPG)

Below: In 2013, JAL introduced the 'JAL Happiness Express' livery on a number of its aircraft. (Alec Wilson Creative Commons Attribution-Share Alike 2.0 Generic https://commons.wikimedia.org/wiki/File:JA772J_%2810513499333%29.jpg)

Some planes used on domestic routes also received the JAL Happiness Express livery. (Jozef Mols collection)

This Boeing 767-300 received the 'Tokyo Olympics and Paralympics 2016' livery. (Amayagan, Creative Commons CC0 1.0 Universal Public Domain Dedication https://commons.wikimedia.org/wiki/File:JapanAirlines_B767-300_fukuoka_20081212132904.jpg)

When this Boeing 787-800 joined the JAL fleet, it immediately received the 'new' flying crane livery, as the airline changed its logo again after emerging from bankruptcy. (Alan Wilson, CC BY-SA 2.0 https://commons.wikimedia.org/wiki/Category:JA839J_(aircraft)#/media/File:Boeing_787-8_%E2%80%98JA839J%E2%80%99_Japan_Air_Lines_(48360103582).jpg)

Chapter 12

Collecting Awards

While JAL was consolidating its new freedom after emerging from bankruptcy, its subsidiary Japan Transocean Air (JTA), a company in which JAL owned 51 per cent of the shares, made a branding change, simply by introducing the 'Whale Shark' livery. The idea did not come from a marketing manager, but from a flight crew member who had visited the Okinawa Churaumi Aquarium and seen many families gazing at the whale sharks. He considered that if whale sharks were flying in the sky, everyone would be excited to see them and kids would be happy too. With this idea in mind, he approached the aquarium. The sales department then took over. Although they agreed with the pilot's ideas, they were unsure of how to realise them, including the design and paint technology. After overcoming numerous obstacles, the project accelerated in earnest and in December 2012, the Whale Jet, modelled after the whale shark 'Jinta' at the Okinawa Churaumi Aquarium, took to the sky.

JAL introduced special liveries of its own. In February 2014, the 'Samurai Blue Support Jet', Boeing 777-200 JA8985, was introduced on domestic routes, followed by a second jet (Boeing 777-300 JA7404), which entered the international circuit. In the meantime, JAL was named winner of the On-Time Performance Service Awards in the Major International Airlines category for the second consecutive year. A few months later, in May, the airline was named best airline in the Traveler's Choice Awards by well-known travel review site TripAdvisor. May also saw JAL introduce newly designed JAL SKY NEXT aircraft on its Haneda–Fukuoka route. The Sakura Lounge in Haneda's airport's international terminal and the new economy seats on domestic flights, equipped with JAL SKY NEXT, would later receive Good Design Awards. In July, the airline began offering in-flight internet service aboard domestic flights and introduced First Class Cabins on its Boeing 767 aircraft flying on domestic routes. Then, in August, it announced its sponsorship of the Japan National Rugby Union team and the Japan National Rugby Sevens team.

There was also more business news to consider. In October, Hokkaido Air Systems Co (HAC) joined the JAL group when JAL took a 57.3 per cent interest in this company. JAL also premiered its 'Pink Ribbon Jet' livery on Boeing 777-200 JA8983 as part of the airline's breast cancer awareness campaign. In collaboration with JR East Group, the 'Suica Penguin Jet' livery was introduced on Boeing 767 jets.

Throughout all of this, the airline continued to collect awards. In January 2015, JAL was named winner of On-Time Performance Service Awards Asia Pacific by FlightStats Inc. That month also saw the airline's environment awareness programme for children, 'Sky Eco Class', receive the Sapporo Ministry Environment Award. In March 2015, JAL was recognised as a 'Nadeshiko Brand', an annual distinction reserved for companies promoting diversity and support for women in the workplace. The airline was also recognised as the first 'Health and Productivity Stock Selection'. JAL's air observation project Contrail received the special award of the 24th Grand Prize for the Global Environment Award. At Skytrax's 2015 World Airline Awards, held in June, JAL received its first Best Economy Class Airline Seat award.

The airline also continued to expand its portfolio of co-operation agreements. In May 2015, JAL signed a corporate marketing partnership with Universal Studios Japan, becoming the company's official airline partner. In June, the airline was named official airline partner of the 2020 Tokyo Olympic and Paralympic Games. As the Japanese government was planning to add more slots at Tokyo's Haneda airport by 2020 in time for the Summer Olympics, the airline considered adding more widebodies to its fleet. It even studied the proposed Boeing New Midsize Airplane. In August, JAL was named official airline of the International Basketball Federation. In October 2015, JAL signed a corporate partnership agreement with Hakuta, operated by ispace, Inc, Japan's first privately developed moon-exploration team. Then, in early 2016, the airline signed an official sponsorship agreement with Japan Tennis Assocation's Japan National Team. The airline also became sponsor of the Japan National Team at the Davis Cup and Fed Cup. And a little later, JAL became an official partner of the Japan Wheelchair Rugby Federation and the Japan Wheelchair Basketball Federation, as well as official carrier of the Sapporo Asian Winter Games.

New liveries also emerged from the airline's paint hangar. The 'FLY JAL to 2020' scheme for domestic routes appeared on Boeing 777-300 JA751J, whereas Boeing 737-800s used on the same routes received the 'JAL Happy Journey Express' livery. In March 2016, JAL unveiled its 'JET-KEI' livery on Boeing 777-300ER JA733J operating the Haneda–London route. By 2015, several new routes had commenced, including Haneda–Guangzhou, Haneda–Shanghai Pudong and Haneda–Dallas. The new Embraer 190 was introduced on the Osaka–Kagoshima route. JAL's paint shop remained busy when JAL introduced the 'JAL Doraemon Jet' livery on the Narita–Shanghai route's Boeing 767-300 JA610J, plus the 'Tokyo 2020 Games' livery, featuring a design shared with competitor ANA. As part of its Kyushu Support Project, JAL applied the 'Visit Kyushu!' livery to 767-300s flying domestic routes.

In 2017, JAL and Boom Supersonic announced a strategic partnership to bring commercial supersonic travel to passengers. Boom was developing a new generation supersonic aircraft intended to fly at Mach 2.2, which would cut flight times in half. Through this agreement, JAL would provide its knowledge and experience as an airline to support Boom in developing the aircraft. JAL made an investment of $10m (£7.58m) in Boom and together embarked upon refining the aircraft design and defining the passenger experience for supersonic travel. The airline also took an option to purchase up to 20 Boom supersonic aircraft through a pre-order arrangement.[1] JAL's interest in supersonic travel was not new; the carrier ordered three Concorde aircraft in its early stages of production, but, in common with many other airlines that had taken options, subsequently cancelled the order.

Shortly after, Japan Air Commuter, the regional subsidiary of JAL, received its first of nine ATR42-600s. At that time, the carrier was using a fleet of nine Bombardier Q400s and nine Saab 340s.[2] In 2018, the airline received its first ATR 72-600.[3] JAL itself started the Haneda to New York route, operated with a Boeing 777-300ER. In April 2017, Dassault Falcon Service and JAL announced a private jet service that would provide airline passengers flying from Tokyo to Paris with seamless interconnection to onward destinations in Europe and Africa. Starting on 1 May 2017, the service would include ground transport between the JAL terminal at Paris Charles de Gaulle airport and the DFS base at Paris Le Bourget. This would allow JAL customers to fly point to point at short notice to hundreds of destinations not covered by its commercial flight network. The DFS-operated service would rely on a fleet of nine Falcon aircraft, including two very long-range Falcon 7X trijets, with a pay-as-you-go all-inclusive pricing structure based on the aircraft type and the distance travelled. At the same time, it was announced that the service might be extended later on to the United States and other JAL markets.[4] In September 2017, JAL announced the launch of a Narita–Melbourne route to be operated by a Boeing 787-8, and a Narita to Kona (Hawaii) service, flown by a Boeing 767-300. On 26 September 2017, JAL and Hawaiian Airlines signed a code-share agreement for a frequent flyer programme partnership that would start on 1 October 2018.

From May to September 2018, to commemorate Amuro's 25th anniversary and her retirement, the image of Amuro promoting her *Namie Amuro 25th Anniversary in Okinawa* appeared on Japan Transocean Air's Boeing 737, which was also known as 'Amuro Jet'. (Comyu Creative Commons Attribution-Share Alike 4.0 International https://commons.wikimedia.org/wiki/File:Japan_Transocean_Air_JA07RK_Boeing_737-8Q3_Amuro_Jet_(Starboard-tail).jpg)

Japan Transocean Air Boeing 737-446 JA8992 received the special 'Whale Shark with Cherries' livery. (lasta 29, Creative Commons Attribution 2.0 Generic license. https://commons.wikimedia.org/wiki/File:Japan_Transocean_Air,_B737-400,_JA8992_%2817825949943%29.jpg)

The idea of painting a Boeing 737 in the 'Whale Shark' livery came from a Transocean Airlines flight crew member. (Alec Wilson Creative Commons Attribution-Share Alike 2.0 Generic license. https://commons.wikimedia.org/wiki/File:JA8939_(1049358 1686).jpg)

A JAL Boeing 777-200 in the Samurai Blue livery. (comyo CC BY-SA 4.0 https://commons.wikimedia.org/wiki/Category:JA8985_(aircraft)#/media/File:JAL_JA8985_Boeing_777-246_Samurai_Blue_Jet_2014_at_Haneda.jpg)

JAL's paint shop was not idle. Here is the Boeing 767 Celebration Express, seen at Haneda in 2019. (Alan Wilson, CC BY-SA 2.0https://commons.wikimedia.org/wiki/Category:JA612J_(aircraft)#/media/File:Boeing_767-346ER_%E2%80%98JA612J%E2%80%99_Japan_Airlines_(Tokyo_Disney_Resort_35th_Anniversary_livery)_(49035605517).jpg)

JAL became the official carrier of the 2020 Olympic Games in Tokyo, which is shown on this Boeing 777 (Errands Department, Creative Commons Attribution-Share Alike 4.0 International license. https://commons.wikimedia.org/wiki/File:JAL_JA773J.jpg)

Above: The 'JET-KEI' livery was introduced on the Haneda–London route, as seen on this Boeing 777-300ER. (Tomas del Coro, CC BY-SA 2.0 https://commons.wikimedia.org/wiki/Category:Jet-Kei#/media/File:JA733J_Japan_Airlines_Boeing_777-346(ER)_s-n_32432_%22JET_KEI%22_(37613734080).jpg)

Left: The 'FLYJAL to 2020' livery was used on Boeing 777-300s flying domestic routes. (Lasta 29, CC BY-SA 2.0 https://commons.wikimedia.org/wiki/Category:JA751J_(aircraft)#/media/File:Japan_Airlines,_B777-300,_JA751J_(19715148005).jpg)

The tenth anniversary of Duffy the Disney Bear at Tokyo Disney Resort was part of the 'JAL Happy Journey Express' livery on this Boeing 737-800, used on domestic routes. (Comyo, Creative Commons Attribution-Share Alike 4.0 International license. https://commons.wikimedia.org/wiki/File:JAL_Express_JA341J_Boeing_737-846_Happy_Journey_Express.jpg)

Top: The JAL 'Doraemon Jet' livery was introduced on routes to China. (N509FZ, CC BY-SA 4.0 https://commons. wikimedia.org/wiki/Category:JA610J_ (aircraft)#/media/File:JA610J@PEK_ (20170511110316).jpg)

Above: The 'Visit Kyushu' livery was used on Boeing 767-300s. (Alec Wilson, CC BY-SA 2.0 https://commons. wikimedia.org/wiki/Category:JA656J_ (aircraft)#/media/File:JA656J_ (43642514584).jpg)

Right: Japan Air Commuter received its first ATR-42-600 aircraft in 2017. (photographer's name unreadable, CC BY-SA 4.0 https://en.wikipedia.org/ wiki/Japan_Air_Commuter#/media/ File:Tajimaairports.ATR_42-600.jpg)

Chapter 13

Expansion by Code-Sharing

After JAL emerged from bankruptcy in 2011, it had little means of expanding its operations in order to stay competitive as a major intercontinental carrier. Code-share agreements with both British Airways and American Airlines in 2011 had been signed, giving JAL the opportunity to increase its destinations without the associated commercial risks. In 2014, a similar agreement was signed with Qatar Airways on the Doha–Tokyo Haneda route, as well as on the Tokyo Narita–Doha and Osaka–Doha routes. When this strategy proved successful, JAL decided to further develop this policy where feasible, as soon as possible.

In February 2017, China Airlines expanded code-share its agreement with JAL, covering all flights operated by both carriers between Japan and Taiwan. Earlier, JAL had started code-sharing with Iberia on the Madrid–Tokyo route.[1] In October 2017, another agreement was announced, between JAL and Aeromexico, stemming from the rapid growth of Japanese manufacturers in Mexico as well as the increase in tourism traffic between both countries. Prior to the signing of the agreement, Aeromexico had started up flights from Mexico City to Narita, whereas JAL offered services to eight Mexican cities through a code-share via Los Angeles and Dallas Fort Worth.[2] In 2018, JAL and Russian carrier S7 expanded their own code-share agreement, with JAL adding the Tokyo Narita–Irkutsk and Narita–Novosibirsk routes to its network.

2018 also saw Garuda Indonesia expand its US routes with a Japan Airlines code-share deal. The Indonesian flag carrier had sought to fly to American destinations on its own for several years, but an inability to obtain landing slots at a Japanese airport for a stopover en route to the USA and subsequent financial constraints thwarted this plan. Therefore, Garuda signed code-share agreements with Delta on a route to Los Angeles via Haneda, and with China Airlines for a route to San Francisco via Taipei. The new code-share agreement with JAL expanded Garuda's American business; Garuda passengers could fly to New York and Los Angeles via Narita airport aboard JAL aircraft. The new agreement also included shared flights between Indonesian and Japanese cities, giving the two airlines greater access to each other's markets. The cities covered under the agreement included Jakarta, Denpasar, Surabaya and Yogyakarta in Indonesia and Tokyo, Fukuoka, Nagoya and Chitose in Japan.[3] In February 2019, JAL announced a code-share partnership with Vistara, a full-service carrier from India. This deal would open up more routes between India and Tokyo than ever before. In co-operation with Vistara, JAL's only code-share partner in India, JAL could add 32 Vistara-operated flights each day across India, covering seven cities including Mumbai, Kolkata, Chennai, Bengaluru, Hyderabad, Ahmedabad and Pune.[4]

In September 2019, Japan Airlines and Aircalin announced a collaboration. Through a code-share agreement, Japan Airlines would offer five weekly flights between Tokyo Narita and Noumea, the capital of New Caledonia, as well as five weekly flights between Noumea and Osaka Kansai. Aircalin, on the other hand, would put its code on flights to major cities in Japan, such as Osaka, Fukuoka, Nagoya and Sapporo.[5] Then, in 2020, JAL and Royal Brunei became partners on routes between Narita and Bandar Seri Begawan, the capital of Brunei.[6] A little later still, Japan Airlines enhanced its international network in China by signing a code-share agreement with Shanghai Airlines, resulting in two new destinations for JAL. Both airlines would co-operate on the Shanghai Pudong–Osaka Kansai route as well as on the Shanghai–Toyama route, with both code-share flights operated by Shanghai Airlines.[7] A few days later, JAL announced a code-share agreement with MIAT Mongolian Airlines, whereby JAL would operate flights between Ulaanbaatar in Mongolia and Tokyo Narita as well as Osaka Kansai. MIAT would simultaneously offer flights beyond Narita to Osaka Itami and Nagoya Chubu, in addition to five international destinations, namely Singapore, Melbourne, Ho Chi Minh City, Hanoi and Busan.[8]

Such agreements, however, did not only apply to passenger services. In 2019, JAL entered into a code-share agreement with Kalitta Air, under the terms of which Kalitta would operate three code-share flights per week between Tokyo Narita and Chicago O'Hare. This way, JAL, which had to suspend its own cargo services as a result of its bankruptcy, could enter the cargo market via the back door. Upon emerging from bankruptcy, it had offered chartered freight services, based upon seasonal demand. As a result of the agreement with Kalitta, JAL could now offer scheduled departures for its cargo flights to the American continent.[9]

JAL did not only focus on co-operation with other carriers to expand its business. In May 2018, JAL announced plans to launch a new international low-cost carrier business for the 2020 summer schedule. This new airline would have to compete with other Asian LCCs, as JAL noticed such carriers were attempting to expand into the Japanese market. One of those competitors was Singapore Airlines, which had set up Scoot Airlines, using Boeing 787 jets. In a first step, JAL established a wholly owned subsidiary with the task of preparing LCC business. This was known at first as TBL Co Ltd (Kabushiki-gaisha Ti Bi Eru, which means 'joint stock company to be launched') and was planned to take to the sky just in time for the 2020 Summer Olympics in Japan. In March 2018, JAL revealed the airline's new name, Zipair, the word 'Zip' referring to speed and 'ZIP code'. Accordingly, TBL was renamed 'Zipair Tokyo Inc'. The new airline commenced with flights to Bangkok and Seoul on 14 May and 1 July 2020 respectively. It was planned that flights to the United States could be added to the route map at a later date.[10] Unfortunately, all these plans would be thrown up in the air.

On 15 January 2020, the first COVID-19 patient in Japan was confirmed, with infections coming in several waves in the following months.[11] This was not the only country confronted with the new pandemic, of course, and many of them closed their borders to foreigners. Thailand, for instance, banned all incoming passenger flights from 4 April 2020, whereas the Japanese government imposed strict border enforcement measures. Under these circumstances, Zipair announced on 9 April that its launch of services would be postponed until further notice. In the meantime, it was announced that the carrier had submitted an application to the Japanese authority for the launch of cargo flights between Tokyo and Bangkok to meet the needs for air cargo during the suspension of passenger flights. This service commenced on 3 June 2020, making use of Zipair's Boeing 787-8.[12]

JAL's first Airbus A350-900 was received on 13 June 2019, of the company's outstanding order for 18 such aircraft plus 13 larger A350-1000s. The first deliveries started operations on the Tokyo Haneda–Fukuoka route. Otherwise, at this point in time, JAL operated a fleet of 50 Boeing 737s, 35 Boeing 767s, 40 Boeing 777s and 42 Boeing 787s.

The Airbus A350 was proudly introduced by JAL. (カテキン Creative Commons Attribution-Share Alike 4.0 International licence https://commons.wikimedia.org/wiki/File:JA02XJ_in_Osaka_Int%27l_Airpotrt_20210403.jpg)

A Japan Airlines Airbus A350-900. (Melv_L - MACASR Creative Commons Attribution-Share Alike 2.0 Generic licensehttps://en.m.wikipedia.org/wiki/File:Japan_Airlines_Airbus_A350-900_JA04XJ_(49165956363).jpg)

JAL also introduced the Airbus A350-1000. (Melvin Loi Creative Commons Attribution-Share Alike 2.0 Generic license. https://en.m.wikipedia.org/wiki/File:Japan_Airlines_A350-1000_JA01WJ.jpg)

Zipair was set up by JAL as a subsidiary in order to compete with low-cost carriers on certain routes. (Zipair)

Right: Arrival of Zipair Boeing 787. (Zipair)

Below: A Zipair Boeing 787. (Melv_L - MACASR Creative Commons Attribution-Share Alike 2.0 Generichttps:// en.wikipedia.org/wiki/File:Zip_ Air_Boeing_787-8_JA822J_ (49429383758).jpg

The Pandemic

With the start of the COVID-19 pandemic, worldwide commercial aviation nearly came to a standstill. Even so, the effects of the pandemic were not the same in all countries. When the first infection was confirmed in Japan on 15 January 2020, various measures to curb the spread of the virus were adopted, although the Japanese government imposed fewer restrictions in general, probably due to the uniqueness of Japanese emergency law where a forced lockdown by order of the government is not permitted. Although the lower level of restrictions should have had less impact on travel, the Japanese domestic passenger market declined sharply in April 2020, bottoming out in June and remained among the weakest of those tracked by IATA in February 2021. The responses of each airline also differed; JAL, ANA, Jetstar Japan and Peach cut their services drastically at the beginning of the pandemic to cope with reduced demand, while Skymark, which had been the third largest carrier before the pandemic, ranked lower than a typical low-cost carrier by the end of 2020.[1]

In April 2020, JAL announced revisions to its flight frequency plans for the month of May, with international services reduced by approximately 97 per cent through 31 May. Domestic services had previously been reduced between 29 March and 5 April 2020, so to keep business operational worldwide, the airline resolved to operate cargo-only flights on select routes.[2] In June 2020, JAL announced that it planned to halve bonuses for employees over the summer months due to the sharp deterioration in business. In the past, the airline had paid two months of wages as a bonus, but expected to cut this to one month's worth. JAL had seen a 98 per cent plunge in the number of international passengers in April from a year earlier to 16,039.[3] Subsequently, the airline also cut profit forecasts by more than 40 per cent and projected that net profit for the fiscal year ending in March would be only 53bn yen (£271m), rather than the earlier forecast of 93bn yen (£476m).[4] Disposals of aircraft now had to be made; in July 2020, JAL retired its first long-range jet when a 17-year-old Boeing 777-200ER was sent to the desert boneyard in Victorville, California. JAL had expected to operate the -200ERs well into the 2020s, having launched a cabin retrofit project in 2016 that gave the jets lie-flat, direct-aisle-access business class seats on flights to South-East Asia and Hawaii.[5] At the same time, however, a company spokesman stated that JAL expected to restore 50 per cent of domestic capacity in August and resume a normal schedule as early as October. Domestic markets, which don't have foreign restrictions or quarantine, were indeed a buffer for airlines; JAL at that time had a 51-49 split of international versus domestic passenger revenue in the nine months to 31 December 2019.[6] With signs of a recovery of travel demand after the lifting by the end of May of a nationwide state of emergency that had seen the airline cut the number of flights offered, JAL intended to increase flight frequencies as of October, additionally using larger aircraft so that fully-booked flights would be avoided as much as possible.[7] However. these plans did not materialise. Although the plunge in airline bookings in April 2020 was followed in early June by the start of a gradual recovery, a second wave of infections emerged in Tokyo in August and travel restrictions were put in place. Domestic weekly seat numbers fell back to the low levels seen in April and JAL and ANA were both compelled to scale back their flights once again.[8]

Although passenger demand disappeared, JAL survived thanks to a shift to cargo transportation. This was a relatively easy transition; even during normal times, passenger aircraft typically carry freight in cargo holds along with luggage. Because of the loss of passenger flights and their associated cargo space, shipping rates had jumped, especially on routes connecting to Shanghai and North America. The freight in this case primarily consisted of semiconductor materials or products related to computers. Without dedicated freight aircraft, JAL started repurposing empty passenger planes as cargo transporters, thus between March and August 2020, JAL operated roughly 1,100 scheduled freight flights. The airline also transported cargo (mainly fresh fish such as tuna) between Tokyo and Brisbane, a route not available to passengers. Meanwhile, Zipair, which had not yet started up passenger flights, launched weekly cargo flights between Tokyo and Bangkok. Demand proved higher than anticipated and Zipair ended up adding two more flights a week.[9]

In an interview with Nikkei Asia, JAL's president explained that COVID forced the airline into a new strategy of reducing its focus on international business travel in order to strengthen its low-cost network. This statement came at a time when many international carriers thought that travel patterns would undergo a permanent shift following the pandemic, with far less of the sort of business travel that has underpinned profits at 'full service' carriers such as JAL, which itself was concerned that demand for business travel would not come back to previous levels. Therefore, the airline would need to leverage low-cost holiday models so as to take into account reduced business demand. According to JAL's president Akasaka, JAL would concentrate low-cost networks around Narita, one of its main hubs, in this way supporting subsidiaries Jetstar Japan and Spring Airlines Japan. Jetstar Japan had suffered through having to halt all of its international flights and reduce more than half of its domestic flights; to save money it offered voluntary retirement or furlough to its nearly 600 pilots and flight attendants. JAL, however, adopted a different policy, relocating flight attendants to region-boosting projects. Several flight attendants, however, were compelled to take temporary work in hospitals or in agriculture instead. At the same time, Akasaka indicated that he would rethink the fleet renewal cycle. JAL replaced nearly ten aircraft every year, but hastening the retirement of other aircraft, including Boeing 777s, and delaying the introduction of new types offered a solution; some aircraft had already been sold. He also confirmed that JAL had received a credit line by borrowing from banks, such as Mizuho and MUFG.[10]

In an effort to support passengers wishing to return to flying, Japan Airlines started offering complimentary COVID-19 coverage for international passengers within the framework of its JAL FlySafe programme. As international flights slowly resumed, the JAL group sought to provide customers a safe and secure travel experience in co-operation with Allianz Travel. The free-of-charge insurance included up to 150,000 euro (£125,000) of coverage for medical costs resulting from the medically necessary COVID-19 testing fee and subsequent medical treatment for those that tested positive during their travels. Additional coverage for isolation costs and repatriation was also included. Furthermore, a global 24-hour support line in English and Japanese was available to assist customers exhibiting symptoms.[11]

Despite earlier hopes of a quick recovery of demand, ANA and JAL had to stop bookings to Japan again in December 2021, in line with a government request to stem the spread of the new Omicron variant of COVID-19. On 2 December, two passengers, one arriving from South America and one from Africa, had been hospitalised with high fever and sore throat, despite being fully vaccinated. As a result, the government decided to refuse access to the country for all foreign passengers. Japan would also deny re-entry to all foreigners, including residents with long-term visas. Furthermore, the government imposed tougher quarantine measures for Japanese citizens who had recently been to certain countries or regions such as South Korea, Australia, Germany, Sweden and Portugal.[12]

The pandemic did not stop airlines from trying to expand their market share. JAL, for example, increased its stake in Spring Airlines Japan to a majority stake in May 2021.[13] Earlier, in February 2020, just before the start of the pandemic, Aeroflot and Japan Airlines had decided to start co-operation on flights between Russia and Japan. Besides flights between Moscow and Tokyo, domestic flights in both countries were also part of the deal, which of course had to be postponed due to the pandemic.[14] A similar joint venture between Malaysia Airlines and Japan Airlines, covering flights between both countries, was delayed for the same reason.[15] At the same time, Air France-KLM and Japan Airlines announced the intention to invest in Malaysian Airlines; JAL was interested in a 25 per cent stake, due to the airline's intention to set up a hub in Kuala Lumpur for its low-cost flights.[16]

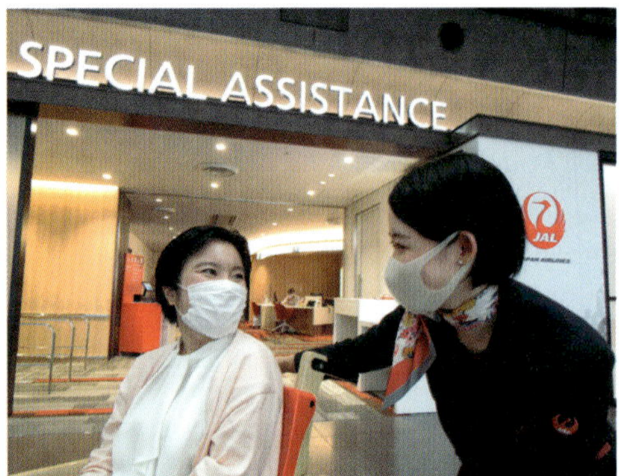

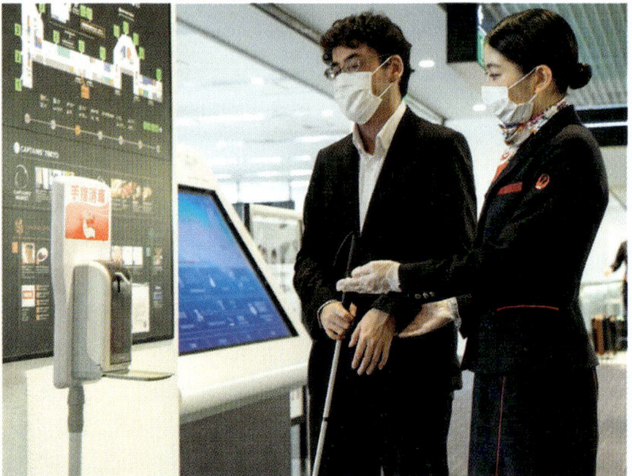

Above left: During the COVID pandemic, JAL did not cancel all its flights and therefore set up a special assistance service for passengers. (JAL)

Above right: COVID prevention during the pandemic. (JAL)

Left: Not only in the aircraft, but also at the airport, JAL put in place a full COVID prevention policy. (JAL)

Below: During the pandemic, JAL increased its participation in Spring Airlines Japan. (Masakatsu Ukon, Creative Commons Attribution-Share Alike 2.0 Generic license. https://commons.wikimedia.org/wiki/File:Spring_Airlines_Japan,_Boeing_737-800_JA02GR_NRT_(17111503868).jpg)

Chapter 15

The Aftermath

The pandemic may have forced JAL to reduce its number of flights, but that didn't mean all activities came to a halt. One of the airline's long-term goals was to achieve net zero CO_2 emissions by 2050, and as a starter, the carrier switched 10 per cent of the total amount of fuel it used to Sustainable Aviation Fuel (SAF), in to keep total emissions below 90 per cent of the amount in fiscal year 2019. On 17 June 2021, JAL conducted the first flight, between Tokyo Haneda and Sapporo, using two different types of SAF loaded at the same time. This fuel was produced locally, at demonstration plants in Japan. Back in 2009, the airline had experimented with SAF made from camelina (a type of non-edible flowering plant), but the project was interrupted due to JAL's bankruptcy. In 2017, SAF was used on a JAL flight from Chicago O'Hare to Narita airport, and in January 2019, this fuel was used on a flight from San Francisco International to Haneda. Upon receipt of Airbus A350 aircraft, SAF was used in all five delivery flights from the Airbus plant in Toulouse to Haneda. In March 2020, Japanese producers managed to manufacture SAF using cotton from old clothing for the first time.[1] By June 2021, both JAL and ANA operated domestic commercial flights from Tokyo Haneda, using sustainable aviation fuel produced in Japan. ANA used microalgae-based SAF, whereas JAL used a fuel derived from wood chips. The new fuels were produced under a project led by the New Energy and Industrial Technology Development agency in co-operation with Toyo Engineering, Mitsubishi Power and Japan Aerospace Exploration Agency (JAXA). In the meantime, JAL had invested in the American SAF producer Fulcrum BioEnergy, and is planning to use SAF on all flights between North America and Japan.[2]

While JAL was experimenting with new fuel types, the airline decided to retire all of its Pratt & Whitney-powered Boeing 777's by March 2021, bringing this forward from the originally planned date of March 2022. This came after an incident with a United Airlines aircraft that experienced a dramatic engine failure during a trip from Denver to Honolulu, when the intake ring fell off. In December 2020, a JAL 777-200 also shed one of the hollow fan blades from its PW4000 engine. Considering the dramatic drop in flight reservations during the ongoing pandemic, this decision did not directly affect operations.[3] JAL had, in fact, announced its resumption of flights between Tokyo Narita and San Diego International Airport. Pre-COVID, the airline had offered daily non-stop flights on this route, but now, only four flights a week were planned.[4]

In early May 2022, JAL said that it expected the recovery of international flights to remain at only 45 per cent of their pre-COVID level for the year 2022, despite Japan's plans to resume accepting foreign tourists. Japan lagged behind other countries at this point when it came to the entry of foreigners, but the government was indeed considering increasing the maximum number of visitors to Japan from 10,000 per day to 20,000. At the same time, JAL's president Yuji Akasaka expressed his hopes that his airline might return to profit for the first time in three years, though he simultaneously feared that domestic flights would recover to only 90 per cent of pre-COVID levels.[5] Even with the increase of passenger numbers to 45 per cent of pre-COVID levels, Japan Airlines' capacity outstripped demand. Indeed, JAL was flying at 65 per cent of its capacity. In the domestic market, the airline was operating at full capacity, though demand was only about 80 per cent of pre-COVID levels.[6]

At this point, JAL's subsidiary Zipair announced a change of livery, by which the large letter Z on the tailfin of its livery would be replaced by a green geometric pattern to avoid misunderstandings, as the letter had been used as a military symbol by the Russian armed forces during the invasion of Ukraine. With a third Boeing 787 (from JAL) in its fleet, Zipair announced the launch of a new Tokyo–San Jose International Airport route to start in December 2022. In April 2023, it also announced new flights to San Francisco International Airport and Manila. By that time, the airline had increased its fleet to seven aircraft, many of them transferred from parent company Japan Airlines.

JAL now decided to introduce three Boeing 767-300ER Freighter aircraft to its fleet. This was the first time in 13 years that the airline had operated its own freighters. In the past, the airline had operated through code-share agreements but, with the cargo business growing, JAL planned a further increase in capacity by operating its own such jets. This decision came in line with the '2024 issue', which refers to a shortage of truck drivers in Japan due to the revision of labour regulations. By adding 767s, JAL could recoup part of the cargo market, until then served by truck services. The same aircraft would also be used on cargo routes within East Asia.[7]

Keeping in line with its policy to reduce CO_2 emissions, JAL signed a Memorandum of Understanding with ZeroAvia on 16 November 2023, to explore development of hydrogen-electric engines to enable clean flight operations on regional routes in Japan. ZeroAvia is developing a hydrogen-electric propulsion system for 40–90-seat regional turboprops, with entry into service planned for 2027. Besides the engine, Japan Airlines and ZeroAvia will collaborate on assessing operational parameters to retrofit hydrogen-electric aircraft for existing and prospective routes, as well as defining pathways for regulation, retrofit operations, hydrogen fuel infrastructure and engine maintenance, repair and overhaul.[8]

In March 2025, JAL stated that it was the latest carrier to return to pre-COVID growth. It expected its 2023 annual accounts, which cover the 12 months to the end of March 2024, to show higher profits than 2019. At the same time, the airline made known its intentions to further expand its fleet by adding new Airbus A350-900s, A321neos and Boeing 787-9s.[9]

When the airline published its accounts two months later, it became clear that the earlier predictions were correct. The company had indeed managed to significantly exceed the previous year's performance in revenue and profit levels, while the number of visitors to Japan exceeded pre-pandemic levels and was 50 per cent higher than the year before. Zipair even managed to more than double the number of foreign passengers. For domestic passengers, efforts to stimulate demand throughout the year, such as promotional campaigns during off-peak seasons, resulted in the growth of passenger numbers by 20 per cent compared to the previous year.[10] Although inbound demand for flights to Japan was increasing, the growth rate remained low for outbound passengers; actually, inbound and outbound demand were still being pulled in opposite directions by the same dynamic. The wide variance between these flows is not hard to explain, as the same factor that is boosting inbound tourism is dampening it outbound. This factor is the relative weakness of the Japanese yen, as compared to other major currencies. This way, visiting Japan became cheaper for foreigners, whereas visits outside Japan became more expensive for Japanese citizens.[11] The international cargo business, despite a declining trend in air cargo demand following the easing of the pandemic, captured robust e-commerce demand and focused on maximising the volume of high-value added cargo, which increased by about 70 per cent compared with fiscal year 2019.[12]

Despite the positive financial results, Japan Airlines' pilots and crew voiced concerns related to safety issues, expressing apprehension about a lack of on-the-job training and difficulties communicating with more senior employees.[13] During the pandemic, many ground handling staff between the ages of 30 and 50 left JAL to try their luck elsewhere, because they didn't see an imminent recovery in the airline industry. This way, the connecting string between veterans and younger staff was broken. The employees who had normally provided informal training to new recruits were gone, and new recruits felt unable to freely ask questions of more senior workers, a situation exacerbated by a culture where seniority-based hierarchy still runs deep. JAL itself confirmed this in its boardroom during a meeting with shareholders. 'We failed to build an environment where ground staff could ensure safety amid various pressures, and that led to a series of incidents', said Munekazu Tachibana, the carrier's vice president of corporate safety and security. In January 2024, a JAL aircraft collided with a coastguard plane on the runway at Haneda airport. In May, at Fukuoka Airport a pilot failed to properly repeat air traffic controller instructions and subsequently moved beyond a stop line, entering the runway without the control tower's clearance. In another incident during the same month, the tips of two JAL planes came into contact at Haneda airport as one was reversing away from the terminal to prepare for take-off while the other was moving forward to enter an adjacent parking spot. The transport ministry said in March 2024 that JAL is facing a challenge securing sufficient captains as many of them, currently in their fifties, are set to retire by around 2025. Overwork, due to shortage of trained staff, may be another contributing factor to the safety issues.

Chapter 16

Looking to the Future

JAL has unveiled its plans to introduce several new aircraft as part of its fleet renewal strategy. International operations were to be bolstered by adding 20 Airbus A350-900s and ten Boeing 787-9s, to be used on routes to North America, Asia and India.[1] These orders were signed during the Farnborough Air Show 2024 and also included another ten options for the Boeing 787-9. Furthermore, during the same airshow, JAL ordered 11 Airbus A321neos.[2] These smaller Airbus aircraft will operate on domestic services within Japan.[3]

To further expand its business, Japan Airlines and Garuda Indonesia entered a revenue-sharing joint venture aimed at strengthening their respective positions in Asia. The carriers were already partners through a codeshare agreement, but the new collaboration would integrate flight schedules and revenue management, functioning as a single entity. The agreement was signed at a time when competitor ANA was working on a similar partnership with Singapore Airlines to counter challenges in the domestic market.[4]

In another move, aimed at increasing international passenger numbers, JAL started offering free domestic tickets to international tourists visiting Japan. When flying to Japan on a stopover, they could take a domestic flight to another destination in the country free of charge. This promotion from the airline, on top of the rather weak Japanese currency, is intended to further encourage tourists to fly JAL.[5]

In January 2024, the tremendous responsibility of guiding JAL through the extremely competitive post-COVID Japanese market was, for the first time in the airline's history, given to a woman. Not only was Mrs Mitsuko Tottori Japan Airlines' first female boss, but she had started her career in aviation as a member of Japan Air System's cabin crew, with which JAL would later merge. Headlines in the Japanese papers ranged from 'first woman' and 'first former flight attendant' to 'unusual' and 'no way'. Out of the last ten men who held the post, seven were educated at the country's top universities, but Mrs Tottori is a graduate from a far less prestigious women-only junior college. Her appointment came a fewweeks after JAL's flight attendants were lauded for the successful evacuation of passengers from a plane that had collided with a Coast Guard aircraft during landing and subsequently burst into flames at the runway at Tokyo's Haneda airport. Minutes after the collision, all 379 passengers of the Airbus A350-900 safely escaped. As a result, the rigorous training of the flight attendants was suddenly in the spotlight. The appointment of Mrs Tottori was only possible after Kazuo Inamori, an elderly retiree and ordained Buddhist monk, exerted transformational influence on the airline. Having been critical of the previous management, Inamori started, during his leadership, to promote from frontline operations, such as pilots and engineers rather than from bureaucratic posts. Prior to Inamori's appointment, many former government officials used to receive golden parachutes into the carrier's boardroom. The appointment of a first female boss to such a high position in JAL was certainly due to the changes that started under Mr Inamori, and was further influenced by the attention that flight attendants received after the much-publicised collision of one of the brand-new Airbus A350s the carrier had received only weeks earlier.[6]

As leading an airline in today's competitive environment is a big challenge that takes a great deal of courage, having experience in dealing with customers will certainly help Mrs Tottori in her role. As a strong customer base is a prerequisite for success, knowing your clients and their needs is of utmost importance.

Accidents and Incidents

(Information from the Aviation Safety Network and Wikipedia)

On 9 April 1952, a Martin 2-0-2 (N90943 *Mokusei*) leased from Northwest Orient Airlines struck Mount Mihara while operating the first leg of a Tokyo–Osaka–Fukuoka service. All 37 people on board were killed, including the four crew members. As the aircraft did not have a cockpit voice recorder or a flight data recorder, the cause of the crash was never determined.

On 30 September 1957, all four engines of a Douglas DC-4 (JA6011 *Unzen*) failed after take-off from Osaka Air Base at an altitude of 300ft (91m). The aircraft force-landed in a rice field. All 57 people on board managed to escape before the aircraft burned out. The cause of the accident was determined as a malfunctioning cross-feed valve.

On 25 April 1961, a Douglas DC-8-32 (JA8003 *Hakone*) was making a standard approach to Tokyo Haneda airport after a flight from San Francisco. The airplane touched down on the wet runway in the vicinity of the ground-controlled approach (GCA) touchdown point, and reverse thrust was applied immediately, with the wheel brakes applied as soon as the nose wheel touched the ground. Ground spoilers and reverse functioned normally and speed fell to 60 knots indicated airspeed (IAS). At this point, reverse thrust was cancelled. Deceleration thereafter was very poor and reverse trust with full power was re-applied. The emergency airbrake system was used, but the aircraft ran off the end of the 8,900ft (2,700m) runway and came to rest after the main gear entered a ditch 9ft (2.7m) wide and 6ft (1.8m) deep. Later, the aircraft was shipped back to the manufacturer in Long Beach, California, where it was repaired as a Series 53 model and received the new registration JA8008 and name *Matsushima*. It returned to service in early 1963.

On 10 April 1962, a Douglas C-54 (JA 6003 *Haruna*) flying from Fukuoka to Tokyo made a wheels-up landing at Osaka. There were no casualties, but the aircraft was damaged beyond repair and was written off.

On 27 February 1965, a Convair 880 (JA8023 *Kaeda*) was performing low-pass training near Iki airport when it suddenly descended fast and struck the runway. The aircraft slid and caught fire.

On 25 December 1965, a Douglas DC-8-33 (JA8006 *Kamakura*) took off from San Francisco International Airport but suffered a contained engine failure on number one engine while climbing through 4,500ft (1,400m). A fire erupted in the area of the number one engine, but was quickly extinguished. The aircraft made a safe emergency landing at Oakland International Airport (CA). The probable cause was a disintegrating engine failure and in-flight fire caused by the failure of maintenance personnel to properly secure the low-pressure compressor section torque ring during engine overhaul.

On 26 August 1966, a Convair 880 (JA8030 *Ginza*, leased from Japan Domestic Airlines) yawed left for unknown reasons after the nose lifted up during a training flight at Haneda Airport. Some 5,249ft (1,600m) into take-off, the number four engine cut out, causing the aircraft to skid off the runway. All four engines separated, as well as the nose and left landing gear. The aircraft caught fire and burned out. All five crew died.

On 5 October 1967, a Beechcraft H18 (JA5137) crashed in a field at Murayama following engine failure while completing a training flight out of Yamagata airport. All four crew survived.

On 22 November 1968, a Douglas DC-8-62 (JA8032 *Shiga*) arrived in the San Francisco area after an uneventful flight from Tokyo. Normal communications were established and the crew was radar-vectored to the Woodside VOR and then to intercept the ILS for runway 28L at San Francisco. The flight crossed the Woodside VOR at 17.16 at approximately 4,000ft, and at 17.18 was cleared to descend to 2,000ft. The flight descended in a constant uninterrupted rate of descent from this time until about six seconds before water impact in San Francisco Bay at 17.24. Despite being on the localiser to the runway centreline, the aircraft contacted the water about 2.5 miles (4km) from the end of runway 28L. There were no injuries to the passengers or crew during the accident and ensuing evacuation, and the aircraft was recovered from the Bay about 55 hours after the accident. Repairs were carried out by United Airlines and the plane was delivered back to JAL on 31 March 1969. The probable cause was determined as improper application of the prescribed procedures to execute an automatic-coupled ILS approach. The deviation from the prescribed procedures was in part due to a lack of familiarisation and infrequent operation of the installed flight director and autopilot system.

On 24 June 1969, a Convair 880 (JA8028 *Kikyo*) was taking off from runway 32R at Moses Lake Grant County International Airport. The power was reduced on the number four engine during take-off, but the aircraft continued to yaw to the right until the number four engine struck the runway. The aircraft slid off the runway and burst into flames, killing three of the five crew members on board. The probable cause was a delayed corrective action during a simulated critical-engine-out take-off manoeuvre, resulting in an excessive sideslip from which full recovery could not be effected.

On 22 February 1970, Keith Sapsford, a teenage boy, climbed into the cargo area of a Douglas DC-8 (JA8031) operating a flight from Sydney to Tokyo. As the plane was taking off, he fell to his death.

On 31 March 1970, a Boeing 727 (JA8315 *Yodo*) was hijacked by the Japanese Red Army while en route from Tokyo to Fukuoka. The nine hijackers released all 122 passengers and seven crew members at Fukuoka airport and then Seoul's Gimpo International Airport before proceeding to Pyongyang Sunan International Airport, where they surrendered themselves to the North Korean authorities.

On 14 June 1972, a Douglas DC-8-53 (JA8012 *Akan*) struck the banks of the Yamuna River, about 12 miles (20km) east of New Delhi's Palam International Airport. The crash killed ten out of 11 crew members and 72 out of 76 passengers, as well as three people on the ground. Japanese investigators claimed that a false glide path signal was responsible for the descent into terrain, while Indian investigators claimed it was caused by the JAL crew's disregard of laid-down procedures and the abandonment of all instrument indications without properly ensuring sighting of the runway.

On 24 September 1972, a Douglas DC-8-53 (JA8013 *Haruna*) en route to Bombay landed at Juhu airport runway 08, instead of Bombay airport runway 09. The aircraft overran the runway into a ditch. The visibility at the time was 1.6 miles (2.5km), decreasing to 0.93 miles (1.5km). There were no injuries, but the aircraft was written off.

On 6 November 1972, a Boeing 727 (registration unknown) was hijacked by a 47-year old male passenger while on a domestic flight from Tokyo to Fukuoka. Brandishing a pistol, he demanded $2m and to be flown to Cuba. The aircraft returned to Tokyo Haneda airport, where a DC-8 plane was being prepared to fly him to Vancouver and on to Cuba. After releasing most hostages, the hijacker wanted to board the DC-8 while holding three crew members hostage. While entering the aircraft, he was overpowered by five police officers.

On 28 November 1972, a Douglas DC-8-62 (JA8040 *Hida*) was ready to fly from Moscow Sheremetyevo Airport to Tokyo. The aircraft took off and climbed to 330ft (100m) with a supercritical angle of attack but lost height abruptly. It hit the ground and burst into flames, with nine of the 14 crew members and 52 of the 62 passengers dying. The probable cause of the accident was the supercritical angle of attack, probably caused by either an inadvertent spoiler extension in flight or a loss of control following a number one or two engine failure due to ice formation in the engine.

On 20 July 1973, a Boeing 747-200B (JA8109) destined for Anchorage was hijacked by there and four men and a woman shortly after leaving Amsterdam, but the accidental explosion of the female hijacker's device killed her. The aircraft landed at Dubai and, after protracted negotiations, took off for Damascus and finally Benghazi, landing there on 23 July. All passengers and crew members were released at the latter, whereupon the aircraft was blown up.

On 12 March 1974, a Boeing 747SP (JA8117) was hijacked at Naha airport by a Japanese man demanding $56 million (£44m) to study biology and geology. He carried a black suitcase that he stated contained a bomb or weapons. Seven hours later, the man was arrested by police officers disguised as airport workers. The suitcase actually contained 16,000 Japanese yen (£85), an airline ticket, a bottle of vitamins, a sweater and a pair of trousers.

On 15 July 1974, a Douglas DC-8 (registration unknown) was hijacked by a male passenger who demanded the release of the leader of the Japanese Red Army. When this demand was not met, he demanded to be flown to Nagoya. After landing there, the hijacker remained on the flight deck with the pilots. Meanwhile, the flight attendants opened an emergency exit to allow the passengers to escape. Police then stormed the aircraft and arrested the hijacker.

In February 1975, a Japan Air Lines flight from Tokyo to Paris, making fuel stops in Anchorage and Copenhagen, saw 196 passengers and one stewardess, out of 343 on board, suffer food poisoning. Of these, 143 became seriously ill and needed hospitalising when the plane reached Copenhagen; 30 were in critical condition. The source of the food poisoning was ham contaminated with staphylococcus from the infected cuts on the fingers of a cook in Anchorage. The ham was used in omelettes stored at a high temperature on the plane instead of being chilled, allowing time for the bacteria to multiply and produce an exotoxin that was not destroyed by cooking. The head of Japan Airlines' catering service in Anchorage comitted suicide shortly afterwards and he was the only fatality of the incident. Fortunately, the pilots of the flight had not eaten the omelettes; if so, they might have become incapacitated themselves.

On 9 April 1975, a Boeing 747SR (registration unknown) was hijacked by a man who pointed a gun at a steward and demanded a ransom of $100,000 (£78,500). After landing at Tokyo, police boarded the aircaft and overpowered the hijacker while he was speaking to the pilot. No-one was injured.

On 16 December 1975, a Boeing 747-200B (JA8122) slid of the north side of the east–west taxiway at Anchorage International Airport during taxi for take-off on runway 06R. The aircraft weathercocked turned into the wind about 70 degrees to port and slid backward down a snow-covered embankment with an average slope of minus 13 degrees, coming to a stop on a heading of 150 degrees on a service road about 250ft (76m) from and 50ft (15m) below the taxiway surface. The probable cause of the accident was the loss of directional control during taxi as a result of ice on the taxiway and strong direct crosswinds. Contributing to the accident were the captain's decision to take off from runway 06R after receiving reports that taxiing conditions were deteriorating. The failure of the airport management to anticipate predictable unsafe icing conditions was also a contributory factor.

On 5 January 1976, a Douglas DC-8-61 (JA8043) was hijacked in Manila by two Filipino passengers armed with pistols and explosives. After negotiations, all but eight passengers were released. The hijackers demanded a free flight to Japan, but when Japanese authorities refused to give the aircraft permission to land, the hijackers surrendered.

On 13 January 1977, a Douglas DC-8-62AF (JA8054) freighter stalled after take-off from Anchorage International Airport and crashed 980ft (300m) past the runway. The aircraft was on a non-scheduled operation and all five occupants on board, including three crew members and two passengers, were killed. The captain began take-off at the wrong position on the runway and this decision was not questioned by fellow crew members. The captain's initial blood alcohol level was 298mg (4.6gr) while the legal limit in Anchorage was 100mg (1.5gr). The probable cause of the accident was a stall that resulted from the pilot's control inputs aggravated by airframe icing while the pilot was under the influence of alcohol. Contributing to the cause of this accident was the failure of other flightcrew members to prevent the captain from attempting the flight, considering his intoxication.

On 27 September 1977, a Douglas DC-8-62H (JA8051) on a flight from Hong Kong to Kuala Lumpur struck a 300ft (91m) hill on approach during a thunderstorm, four miles (6.4km) short of the runway while on a VHF Omnidirectional Range (VOR) approach to the runway. The fatalities included eight crew members and 26 passengers out of 79 people on board. The accident was caused by the captain descending below minimum descent altitude without having the runway in sight, and continuing the descent until the aircraft struck terrain. A subsidiary contributory factor was insufficient monitoring of the aircraft's flight path by the captain under the adverse weather conditions with several aircraft in the holding pattern awaiting their turn for approach and, more importantly, the co-pilot's failure to challenge the captain's breach of company regulations.

On 28 September 1977, a Douglas DC-8 was hijacked by the Japanese Red Army (JRA) en route from Paris to Tokyo with 156 people on board. The aircraft made a scheduled stop in Bombay and, shortly after taking off from here, five armed JRA members hijacked the aircraft and ordered it to be flown to Dhaka in Bangladesh. Upon arrival, the hijackers held the passengers and crew hostage while demanding $6m (£4.7m) and the release of nine imprisoned JRA members. A chartered JAL flight carried the money and six of the nine imprisoned JRA members to Dhaka, where the exchange took place. The hijackers released all the hostages.

On 2 June 1978, a Boeing 747SR (JA8119) suffered a tailstrike while landing at Osaka. Two passengers were seriously injured and another 23 suffered minor injuries. Although the aircraft was repaired in June and July 1978, it was lost on 12 August 1985 after crashing into Mount Takamagahara with the loss of 520 passengers and crew.

On 23 November 1979, a JAL McDonnell Douglas DC-10 was hijacked shortly after take-off from Osaka by a male passenger. Brandishing plastic knife and a bottle opener, he demanded to be flown to the Soviet Union. The aircraft diverted to Narita airport to refuel, where the hijacker was overpowered before the aircraft was refueled.

On 9 February 1982, a McDonnell Douglas DC-8 was on a scheduled flight from Fukuoka to Tokyo. The aircraft crashed on approach into the shallow waters of Tokyo Bay some 1,670ft (510m) short of the runway 33R threshold. The nose and right wing separated from the fuselage. Among the 166 passengers and eight crew members, 24 passengers were killed. The report later showed that the captain experienced some form of mental aberration although doctors had declared him fit to fly earlier. He was prosecuted, but not found guilty by reason of insanity.

On 17 September 1982, a McDonnell Douglas DC-8-61 (JA8048) took off from Shanghai. Nine minutes after take-off, the crew heard a noise coming from the lower middle part of the aircraft. This was immediately followed by a hydraulic low-level warning, a hydraulic reservoir air low-pressure warning, a complete loss of hydraulic system pressure, abnormal flap position indications and a complete loss of air brake pressure. The crew decided to return to Shanghai for an emergency landing on runway 36. The aircraft overran the runway and came to a rest in a drainage ditch. There were no casualties.

On 12 August 1985, a Boeing 747SR (JA8119) crashed into Mount Takamagahara near Gunma Prefecture. The aircraft was a short-range variant of the Boeing 747 Series 100, specifically configured for domestic flights with a high-density seating arrangement. This particular aircraft had already been involved in an earlier accident in 1978, when it sustained substantial damage to the rear underside of the fuselage. The rear pressure bulkhead was also cracked. It was subsequently repaired by Boeing engineers, who replaced the lower part of the rear fuselage and a portion of the lower half of the bulkhead. Seven years later, on 12 August 1985, the plane had completed four domestic flights when it landed at Tokyo-Haneda. The next flight was to be flight 123 to Osaka, and the aircraft took off from Tokyo-Haneda at 18.12. Twelve minutes later, while climbing through 23,900ft at a speed of 300 knots, an unusual vibration occurred. An impact force raised the nose of the aircraft and control problems were experienced. A decompression had occurred and the crew was alerted to indications of problems with the R5 door. In fact, the rear pressure bulkhead had ruptured, causing serious damage to the rear of the plane. A portion of its vertical fin, measuring 16ft (5m), together with the section of the tailcone containing the auxiliary power unit, was ripped off the aircraft. Due to the damage, the hydraulic pressure dropped and ailerons, elevators and yaw damper became inoperative. Control became very difficult as the aircraft experienced Dutch rolls and phugoid oscillations (unusual movement in which altitude and speed change significantly in a 20-100 second cycle without change of angle of attack). The aircraft started to descend to 6,600ft while the crew tried to maintain control by using engine thrust. Upon reaching 6,600ft, the airspeed had dropped to 108 knots. The aircraft then climbed with a 39-degree pitch-up to a maximum of approximately 13,400ft and started to descend again. At 18.56, JAL123 finally brushed against a tree-covered ridge, continued and struck the Osutaka Ridge, bursting into flames.

Crash investigators wrote, 'It is estimated that this accident was caused by deterioration of flying quality and loss of primary flight control functions due to rupture of the aft pressure bulkhead of the aircraft and the subsequent ruptures of a part of the fuselage tail, vertical fin and hydraulical flight control systems. The reason why the aft pressure bulkhead was ruptured in flight is estimated to be that the strength of the said bulkhead was reduced due to fatigue cracks propagating at the spliced portion of the bulkhead's webs, to the extent that it became unable to endure the cabin pressure in flight at that time. The initiation and propagation of the fatigue cracks are attributable to the improper repairs of the said bulkhead conducted in 1978, and it is estimated that the fatigue cracks having not been found in the later maintenance inspection is contributive to their propagation, leading to the rupture of the bulkhead.' In the crash, 520 of the 524 people on board died. It was at that time the deadliest single-aircraft accident in history.

On 17 November 1986, the crew of a Boeing 747-200F en route to Tokyo informed the air traffic controller in Anchorage that they had seen two Unidentified Flying Objects at the Reykjavik to Anchorage section of the flight. Other aircraft crews were subsequently requested to look for such UFOs, but no reports were received.

On 2 October 1991, a Boeing 747-200B (JA8161) was climbing through FL165 when the force from a hot liquid, released from a burst pipe in the pressurisation system, blew a 3.3 x 2.3ft (100 x 70cm) hole in the fuselage beneath the portside wing. The captain dumped fuel and returned safely to Tokyo.

On 31 March 1993, a Boeing 747-100 (N473EV) operated by Evergreen International Airlines, on behalf of JAL, experienced severe turbulence at an altitude of about 2,000ft (610m) after departure. This resulted in dynamic multi-axis lateral loadings that exceeded the ultimate lateral load-carrying of the number two engine pylon. The number two engine separated from the aircraft, but the number one engine was maintained at emergency/maximum power and the aircraft landed safely back at Anchorage International Airport.

On 8 June 1997, a McDonnell Douglas MD-11 (JA8580) from Hong Kong to Nagoya descended through approx 17,000ft (5,200m) over the Shima Peninsula for an approach to Nagoya. It then experienced abrupt and abnormal altitude changes caused by turbulence, and five passengers and seven crew members were injured. The captain had switched on the 'fasten seatbelt' sign in time, but the passengers who had been injured had ignored this instruction. Nevertheless, the captain was indicted for an alleged error in piloting the MD-11 and then blamed for the death of a cabin crew member 20 months after the incident. However, on 31 July 2004, the Nagoya District Court acquitted the 54-year-old captain.

On 31 January 2001, two JAL aircraft (flight 907, a Boeing 747-400D and flight 958, a McDonnell Douglas DC-10) were involved in a near-miss incident near Yaizu, Shizuoka.

On 12 November 2001, a Boeing 747-400 en route to Tokyo from New York JFK produced wake turbulence that was the initiating factor in the loss of American Airlines flight 587. This was not the fault of JAL and it had no effect on the JAL flight.

On 7 January 2013, ground workers noticed smoke coming out of the battery compartment in a parked Boeing 787 Dreamliner at a gate at Logan International Airport in Boston. There was nobody inside the aircraft at that time. The fire was caused by overcharged lithium-ion batteries, eventually leading to the grounding of the worldwide Boeing 787 fleet and subsequent redesign of the battery systems.

On 28 October 2018, JAL pilot Katsutoshi Jitsukawa was arrested at Heathrow Airport for being under the influence after failing a breathalyser test. He was found to have 189mg of alcohol per 100ml of blood in his system in breach of the 20mg legal limit for pilots. The driver of a crew bus smelled alcohol on the pilot, who was supposed to be part of the crew flying to Tokyo, and alerted the police. The flight took off after a 69-minute delay, and the pilot subsequently pleaded guilty to exceeding the alcohol limit.

On 4 December 2020, a Boeing 777-200 (JA8978) on a flight from Okinawa to Tokyo suffered a fan blade failure in one of its two PW4084 engines. None of the occupants were injured in the incident.

On 2 January 2024, an Airbus A350-941 (JA13XJ) from Sapporo was landing at Tokyo-Haneda airport but collided with a Japan Coast Guard DHC-8 on the runway. Both aircraft caught fire and were written off. All 379 occupants aboard the JAL flight were evacuated, while five of the six crew members aboard the Coast Guard aircraft were killed, the pilot escaping with critical injuries. The Dash 8 had been waiting to depart to Niigata to deliver supplies in response to the Noto Peninsula earthquake.

The wreckage of JA13XJ, the airplane involved in the 2024 Haneda airport runway collision. This photo was taken on the following day from the viewing deck at Haneda Airport Terminal 2. (Makochan12.9, CC BY-SA 4.0) https://simple.wikipedia.org/wiki/2024_Haneda_Airport_runway_collision#/media/File:Japan_Airlines_516_JA13XJ_wreckage.jpg)

Fleet Details

Based on en.wikipedia.org, planespotters.net and JAL Japan Airlines figures.

Aircraft type	Total	Introduction	Last removal	Remarks
Douglas DC-3	1	1951	1951	Leased from Philippine Airlines for three days of promotional tours prior to the start up of the airline
Martin 202	5	1951	1952	Leased from Northwest Airlines
Douglas DC-4	3	1952	1964	
Douglas DC-6B	?	1954	1969	
Douglas DC-7C	5	1958	1965	
Douglas DC-8-30	4	1960	1975	
Convair 880	9	1961	1971	
Douglas DC-8-50	16	1962	1982	
Boeing 727-100	23	1964	1988	
Douglas DC-8-60	38	1968	1988	Including Douglas DC-8-60F
Beechcraft H 18	?	1969	?	Used for pilot training
NAMC YS-11	12	1969	1970	
Boeing 747-100	20	1970	2006	JAL was the launch customer
Boeing 747-200	39	1971	2009	Including freight versions
McDonnell Douglas DC-10-40	17	1976	2005	Also operated by Jalways and Japan Aircharter
Boeing 747-300	19	1984	2009	
Boeing 747-SR	7	1986	2006	
Boeing 767-200	5	1986	2011	
Boeing 747-400	45	1990	2011	Including freighter versions
McDonnell Douglas MD11	10	1993	2004	
Boeing 737-400	7	1995	2003	
Saab 340B	10	1998	2023	Operated by Hokaido Air Service
Bombardier DHC 8	5	1996	current	First delivered to Amakusa Airlines, later taken over by JAL
Boeing 777-300	46	1998	Current	
Bombardier CRJ 200	9	2000	2018	Operated by J-Air
Boeing 777-200	27	2002	2023	

Aircraft type	Total	Introduction	Last removal	Remarks
McDonnell Douglas MD-81	11	2006	2010	After merger with JAS
McDonnell Douglas MD-87	8	2006	2008	After merger with JAS
McDonnell Douglas MD-90	16	2006	2013	After merger with JAL
Airbus A300-600R	22	2006	2011	After merger with JAL
Boeing 767-300ERF	27	2007	current	A few still active
Boeing 737-800	62	2007	current	
Embraer 170	18	2008	current	Operated by J Air
Airbus A320	2	2012		Operated by Jetstar Japan
Boeing 787-8	31	2012	current	
Boeing 787-9	22	2015	current	
Embraer 190	14	2016	current	Operated by J Air
ATR 42-600	13	2017	current	Operated by Japan Air Commuter
ATR 72-600	2	2018	current	Operated by Japan Air Commuter
Airbus A350-900	15	2019	current	
Airbus A350-1000	3	2023	current	
Airbus A321 ceo	3	2023	current	Operated by Spring Japan

Appendix 3

Notes and References

Chapter 1

1. 'Japan', en.wikipedia.org.
2. 'Japanese aviation still soaring after a century. A trailblazer in the country's aeronautics, the University of Tokyo continues its pioneering R&D role today', www.u-tokyo.ac.jp/focus/en/features/f 00031, 15 August 2012.
3. ibid
4. ibid
5. 'Aviator Bud Mars, Japan c. 1911', Dave Rogers, MyBayCity.com, 2012.
6. ibid
7. 'Air Mail flying contest commemorative postcards 1920–1921', Camille Allaz, www.oldtokyo.com, 2005.
8. 'Tokyo–Osaka–Tokyo Air Race 1920', article from 'The Airplane', 16 June 1920, published on www.oldtokyo.com
9. 'Air Mail flying contest commemorative postcards 1920–1921', Camille Allaz, www.oldtokyo.com, 2005.
10. 'East West regular airline', ja.wikipedia.org
11. 'Tokyo Air Transport Company', ja.wikipedia.org
12. 'Japan Air Transport Corporation', en.wikipedia.org
13. Japan Air Transport Co Hinazuru type Airspeed As 6 Envoy 1936', www.oldtokyo.com/japan-air-transport-co-airspeed_as_6-envoy-1936.
14. 'Manchukuo National Airways', ja.wikipedia.org
15. 'Japan Air Transport Corporation', en.wikipedia.org
16. 'Early Japanese civil aviation', www.century-of-flight.net

Chapter 2

1. 'The ban on Japanese aircraft pilots 1945–1952', Matthew Wills, 8 January 2024, https://daily.jstor.org
2. 'Tales of the Dancing Crane – The story of JAL Part 1', Jozef Mols, *Aviation News*, February 2021, Key Publishing Ltd.
3. Ibid
4. ibid
5. ibid
6. 'JAL Japan Airlines', en.wikipedia.org
7. 'Tales of the Dancing Crane – The story of JAL Part 1', Jozef Mols, *Aviation News*, February 2021, Key Publishing Ltd.
8. Https://www.jal.com/en/company/aircraft.

Chapter 3

1. 'All Nippon Airways CO, LTD', en.wikipedia.org
2. 'List of defunct airlines of Japan', en.wikipedia.org
3. 'All Nippon Airways CO, LTD', en.wikipedia.org
4. 'JAL Japan Airlines', en.wikipedia.org
5. ibid
6. 'Air Transport Policy in Japan', Hirotaka Yamauchi and Ito Takatoshi, Institute for International Economics, Washington DC, November 1996.
7. ibid
8. ibid
9. 'Tales of the Dancing Crane – The story of JAL Part 1', Jozef Mols, *Aviation News*, February 2021, Key Publishing Ltd.

Chapter 4

1. 'Corruption, crime and All Nippon's Tristars', 3 March 2015, www.yesterdaysairlines.com
2. 'Throwback: the bribery scandal concerning Japan & the Lockheed Tristar', Justin Surette, 26 April 2023, simpleflying.com
3. 'Corruption, crime and All Nippon's Tristars', 3 March 2015, www.yesterdaysairlines.com
4. 'Tales of the Dancing Crane – The story of JAL Part 1', Jozef Mols, *Aviation News*, February 2021, Key Publishing Ltd.
5. ibid

Chapter 5

1. 'Air Transport Policy in Japan', Hirotaka Yamauchi and Ito Takatoshi, Institute for International Economics, Washington DC, November 1996.
2. ibid
3. 'JAL's History, About Us', JAL website, https://www.jal.com/en/company/jal_history/index_1981s.html

Chapter 6

1. JAL Japan Airlines', en.wikipedia.org
2. 'Tales of the Dancing Crane – The story of JAL Part 1', Jozef Mols, *Aviation News*, Febuary 2021, Key Publishing Ltd.
3. 'JAL Japan Airlines', jp.wikipedia.org

Chapter 7

1. 'Boeing delivers Japan Airlines' first 777-300', Boeing Media Room, 28 July 1998.
2. 'A relentless drive to achieve higher goals', JAL, *JAL Annual Report, 1999.*
3. ibid
4. 'Hokkaido Air System', en.wikipedia.org
5. 'Harlequin Air', en.wikipedia.org
6. 'Skymark Airlines', en.wikipedia.org
7. 'Air Do', en.wikipedia.org
8. 'Amakusa Airlines', en.wikipedia.org
9. 'Japan Airlines Purchases New Boeing 777 and 767 Jetliners', Boeing media room, 27 November 2000.
10. 'JAL Dream Express', ja.wikipedia.org

Chapter 8

1. 'Air Do', en.wikipedia.org
2. 'An Airline Merger and its Remedies: JAL-JAS of 2002', Naoshi Doi and Hiroshi Ohashi, The Research Institute of Economy, Trade and Industry, www.rieti.go.jp/en
3. 'JAL, JAS to merge to beat aviation slump', *The Japan Times*, 13 November 2001.
4. 'Japan Airlines and Japan Air System take a merger move', Ken Belson, *New York Times*, 13 November 2001.
5. 'Japanese carriers JAL, JAS page way for merger', David Jonas, *Business Travel News*, 20 January 2002.
6. 'JAL, JAS give merger details', *The Japan Times*, 30 January 2002.
7. 'ANA files complaint against the proposed merger between JAL and JAS', *Airline Industry Information*, 21 December 2001.
8. 'JAL, JAS merger thrown in doubt', *Airfinance Journal*, March 2002.
9. 'Japan airlines' merger faces challenge', CNN.com, 14 March 2002.
10. 'An airline merger in Japan: a case study revealing principles of Japanese merger control', Kokai Arai, *Journal of Industry*, 2004.
11. 'Merger approved for JAL and JAS', www.travelweeklyweb.com, 29 April 2002.
12. 'Feu vert à la fusion entre JAL et JAS', *L'Echo Touristique*, 29 April 2002.
13. 'Tales of the Dancing Crane – The story of JAL Part 1', Jozef Mols, *Aviation News*, February 2021, Key Publishing Ltd.
14. 'JAS', en.wikipedia.org

15. ibid
16. 'JAL to merge domestic and international operations next year', 6 October 2005, ATWonline.com
17. 'Tales of the Dancing Crane – The story of JAL Part 1', Jozef Mols, *Aviation News*, February 2021, Key Publishing Ltd.
18. 'JAL cancels flights due to engine cracks', Reuters, 19 January 2004.
19. 'Harlequin Air', en.wikipedia.org
20. 'J-Air', en.wikipedia.org
21. 'JAL slashes profit outlook', CNN.com, 12 March 2003.

Chapter 9

1. 'JAL', en.wikipedia.org
2. 'JAL', ja.wikipedia.org
3. 'JAL', en.wikipedia.org
4. ibid
5. 'Tales of the Dancing Crane – The story of JAL Part 1', Jozef Mols, *Aviation News*, February 2021, Key Publishing Ltd.
6. 'J-Air', en.wikipedia.org
7. 'Galaxy Airlines Co Ltd', en.wikipedia.org
8. 'Ibex Airlines', en.wikipedia.org
9. 'Air Next Co, Ltd', en.wikipedia.org
10. 'StarFlyer Inc', en.wikipedia.org

Chapter 10

1. 'Tales of the Dancing Crane – The story of JAL Part 1', Jozef Mols, *Aviation News*, February 2021, Key Publishing Ltd.
2. JAL', en.wikipedia.org
3. Toyama, Kazuhiko, 'The real story of the problems at Japan Airlines', Kazuhiko Toyama, *Global Asia*, 19 January 2010.
4. 'JAL to cut staff, overseas flights: reports', Reuters, 15 September 2009.
5. 'The real story of the problems at Japan Airlines', Kazuhiko Toyama, *Global Asia*, 19 January 2010.
6. ibid
7. 'Air France-KLM in talks to invest in JAL – source', Reuters, 15 September 2009.
8. 'Jal's partners trying to keep it close', CBC News, 18 September 2009.
9. 'Oneworld partners may team for JAL offer', Joseph Woelfel, thestreet.com, 18 September 2009.
10. 'JAL dumps AA, defects to Delta, Skyteam', Linda Hohnholz, ETN eturbonews.com, 29 January 2010.
11. 'Shares in Japan Airlines soar on takeover speculation', CBC News, 14 September 2009.
12. 'Scenarios – Japan airline's fate in hands of task force', Reuters, 30 September 2009.
13. ibid
14. 'JAL boss opposed bankruptcy fix', Takuya Sumikawa, Asahi.com, 4 January 2010.
15. '10 years after corporate near-death experience, Japan Airlines looks to expand', *The Mainichi*, 19 January 2020.
16. 'Japan Airlines and American Airlines strengthen partnership and apply for approval of antitrust immunity', JAL group press communication, 9 February 2010.
17. 'Bankruptcy, Yen 700 billion in public funds eyed for JAL', *The Japan Times*, 8 January 2010.
18. 'Japan Airlines', en.wikipedia.org
19. 'ANA and JAL both report massive load factor improvements on international services in 2010: ANA grows market share'. Anna.aero, 4 August 2010.
20. 'Japan turnaround body picks underwriters for JAL stake sale', Reuters, 15 July 2011.
21. 'JAL', en.wikipedia.org

Chapter 11

1. 'JAL group re-establishes identity with corporate policy and logo change to reflect the commitment and determination of a New JAL', JAL press information, 19 January 2011.
2. 'British Airways and Japan Airlines have agreed a revenue-sharing deal', Toby Melville, Reuters, 12 May, 2011.

3. 'Finnair to tighten British Airways – Japan Airlines tie-up', Robert Wall, Bloomberg.com/news 1 July 2013.
4. 'Japan Airlines and American Airlines announce joint business benefits for Trans Pacific passengers', press release American Airlines, 11 January 2011.
5. 'Finnair to tighten British Airways – Japan Airlines Tie-up', Robert Wall, Bloomberg.com/news 1 July 2013.
6. 'Jetstar Japan Co, Ltd', en.wikipedia.org
7. 'Historische deal tussen Airbus en Japan Airlines', Kevin Van Der Auwera, *Trends*, 10 July 2013.
8. 'Joint press conference with Mitsubishi Aircraft Corporation August 28, 2014', JAL press release, 28 August 2014.
9. 'JAL', en.wikipedia.org

Chapter 12

1. 'Japan Airlines to invest $10m in U.S. Supersonic airline boom,' Bart Noeth, Aviation24.be, 5 December 2017.
2. 'Japan Air Commuter ontvangt eerste ATR42-600', luchtvaartnieuws.nl, 23 January 2017.
3. 'Japan Air Commuter neemt eerste ATR 72-600 in ontvangst', Klaas-Jan van Woerkom, Luchtvaartnieuws.nl, 30 October 2018.
4. 'JAL, Dassault Falcon Service to offer private jet service', Joint Press release JAL and Dassault, 18 April, 2017.

Chapter 13

1. 'China Airlines expands codeshare flights with Japan Airlines', Craig Bright, businesstraveller.com, 21 February 2017.
2. 'Aeromexico and Japan Airlines Announce Codeshare Agreement', JAL group press release, 11 October 2017.
3. Maulia, Erwida, 'Garuda expands US routes with Japan Airlines code-share deal', Nikkei Asia, 6 September 2018.
4. 'Japan Airlines and Vistara enter Codeshare Partnership', JAL group press release, 22 February 2019.
5. 'Japan Airlines and Aircalin announce codeshare agreement', JAL group press release, 12 September 2019.
6. 'JAL begins code sharing with Royal Brunei Airlines', JAL group press release, 5 February 2020.
7. 'Japan Airlines enhances international network in China by signing codeshare agreement with Shanghai Airlines', JAL group press release, 9 January 2020.
8. 'Japan Airlines and MIAT Mongolian Airlines agree on codeshare agreement effective March 31, 2020', JAL group press release, 5 February 2020.
9. 'Japan Airlines announces freighter codeshare agreement with Kalitta Air', JAL group press release, 1 August 2019.
10. 'Zipair', en.wikipedia.org
11. 'Japanese aviation market performance during the COVID-19 pandemic. Analyzing airline yield and competition in the domestic market', Kam To Ng, Xiaowen Fu, Shinya Hanaoka, Tae Hoon Oum, sciencedirect.com, Volume 116, February 2022.
12. 'Zipair', en.wikipedia.org

Chapter 14

1. 'Japanese aviation market performance during the COVID-19 pandemic. Analyzing airline yield and competition in the domestic market', Kam To Ng, Xiaowen Fu, Shinya Hanaoka, Tae Hoon Oum, sciencedirect.com, Volume 116, February 2022
2. 'Japan Airlines revises May 2020 international schedule in response to COVID-19', JAL group press release, 29 April 2020.
3. 'Japan Airlines Co. plans to halve bonuses for its employees', KyodoNews, 2 June 2020.
4. 'Japanese airlines cuts profit forecast more than 40 per cent as virus bites', *Arab News*, 19 July 2020.
5. 'Japan Airlines retires first long-range jet during coronavirus travel downturn', Will Horton, forbes.com, 7 July 2020.
6. 'JAL to fully resume domestic flights as early as October', japantimes.co.jp, 2 July 2020.
7. 'JAL to fully resume domestic flights as early as October', https://english.kyodonews.net/news
8. 'Latest COVID-19 spike quashes japan's domestic air travel rebound', centreforaviation.com, 18 January 2021.
9. 'With few passengers, ANA and JAL haul cargo to stay aloft', Keigo Yoshida and Masashi Isawa, asia.nikkei.com, 6 September 2020.

10. 'COVID forces Japan airlines onto new flight path, president says', Eri Sugiera, asia.nikkei.com, 5 October 2020.
11. 'A Japanese First: Japan Airlines to offer complimentary COVID-19 coverage for international passengers', JAL group press release, 11 December 2020.
12. 'ANA, JAL stop flight bookings to Japan amid Omicron variant fears', english.kyodonews.net, 2 December 2021.
13. 'Japanese aviation market performance during the COVID-19 pandemic. Analyzing airline yield and competition in the domestic market', Kam To Ng, Xiaowen Fu, Shinya Hanaoka, Tae Hoon Oum, sciencedirect.com, Volume 116, February 2022.
14. 'Aeroflot en Japan Airlines gaan nauw samenwerken op vluchten tussen Rusland en Japan', Klaas-Jan van Woerkom, luchtvaartnieuws.nl, 10 February 2020.
15. 'De geplande joint venture tussen Malaysia Airlines en Japan Airlines', Klaas-Jan van Woerkom, luchtvaartnieuws, 10 July 2020.
16. 'Air France-KLM en Japan Airlines behoren to de partijen die een belang willen nemen in Malaysia Airlines', Niek Vernooij, luchtvaartnieuws.nl, 21 January 2020.

Chapter 15

1. 'Project of SAF produced domestically in Japan has succeeded', JAL group press release, 18 June 2021.
2. Surgenor, Christopher, 'Japan Airlines and ANA operate SAF flights with fuels made from wood chips and microalgae', greenairnews.com, 22 June 2021.
3. 'Phelps, Mark, 'Japan Airlines gives P&W powered B777s early retirement', avweb.com, 6 April 2021.
4. Piccolo, Sabrina, 'Japan Airlines announces resumption of nonstop flights to Tokyo from San Diego International Airport', San Diego International Airport press release, 12 January 2021.
5. Taguchi, Shoichiro, 'JAL sees international flights recovering to 45% op pre-COVID level', Asia.nikkei.com, 6 May 2022.
6. 'Japan Airlines' capacity outstrips demand amid COVID curbs, official says', Reuters, 13 September 2022.
7. 'JAL to introduce first freighter in 13 years under new business model', statttimes.com, 4 May 2023.
8. 'Japan Airlines and ZeroAvia to partner in exploring hydrogen electric flights in Japan', ZeroAvia press release, 16 November 2023.
9. Percival, Geoff, 'Japan Airlines latest carrier to return to pre-COVID growth', ittn.ie, 25 March 2024.
10. 'JAL group announces consolidated financial results for the fiscal year 2023', JAL group press release, 2 May 2024.
11. 'Japanese Airline update: JAL and ANA target winter gains as inbound demand soars', Capa Centre for Aviation, 30 August 2024.
12. 'JAL group announces consolidated financial results for the fiscal year 2023', JAL Group press release, 2 May 2024.
13. Singh, Supriya, 'Japan Airlines pilots and crew voice concerns amid recent safery issues', japantimes.co.jp, 26 June 2024.

Chapter 16

1. Orban, André, 'Japan Airlines had unveiled plans to introduce 42 new aircraft', Aviation24.be, 21 March 2024.
2. 'Dunn, Graham, 'Farnborough air show order tracker 2024', flightglobal.com, 23 July 2024.
3. Noëth, Barth, 'Japan Airlines signs order for 20 A350-900s and 11 A321neos', Aviation24.be, 23 July 2024.
4. Orban, André, 'Japan Airlines and Garuda Indonesia to form joint venture to expand Asian market presence', Aviation24.be, 1 October 2024.
5. Cvora, Joe, 'Japan Airlines launches free domestic flights for international passengers', AeroXplorer.com, 17 September 2024.
6. Oi, Mariko, 'The ex-flight attendant who became the first female boss of Japan Airlines', bbc.com/news/business, 26 April 2024.

Other books you might like:

Airlines Series,
Vol. 7

Airlines Series,
Vol. 9

Airlines Series,
Vol. 11

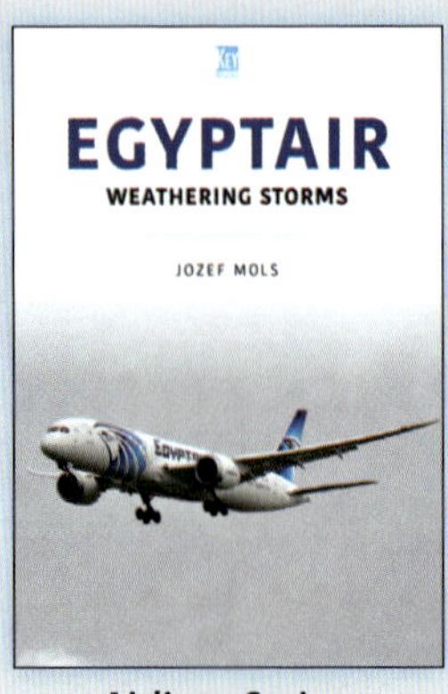

Airlines Series,
Vol. 14

Airlines Series,
Vol. 16

Airlines Series,
Vol. 23

For our full range of titles please visit:

shop.keypublishing.com/books

VIP Book Club

Sign up today and receive
TWO FREE E-BOOKS

Be the first to find out about our forthcoming
book releases and receive exclusive offers.

Register now at **keypublishing.com/vip-book-club**

Our VIP Book Club is a 100% spam-free zone, and we will never share your email with anyone else.
You can read our full privacy policy at: privacy.keypublishing.com